LECTURING
CASE STUDIES, EXPERIENCE AND PRACTICE

EDITED BY
HELEN EDWARDS, BRENDA SMITH AND GRAHAM WEBB

CASE STUDIES OF TEACHING IN HIGHER EDUCATION

KOGAN PAGE

First published in 2001

Kogan Page Limited
120 Pentonville Road
London
N1 9JN
UK

Stylus Publishing Inc.
22883 Quicksilver Drive
Sterling
VA 20166-2012
USA

British Library Cataloguing in Publication Data

A CIP record for this book is available from the British Library.

Paperback: ISBN 0 7494 3519 4
Hardback: ISBN 0 7494 3531 3

Typeset by Saxon Graphics Ltd, Derby
Printed and bound in Great Britain by Biddles Ltd, Guildford and King's Lynn

CONTENTS

CONTRIBUTORS

Marilyn Baird is Head of Radiography and Medical Imaging in the Faculty of Medicine, Nursing and Health Sciences at Monash University, Melbourne, Australia (e-mail: marilyn.baird@med.monash.edu.au).

Sally Brown is Director of Membership Services at the Institute for Learning and Teaching, UK and is Visiting Professor in Assessment at the Robert Gordon University, Aberdeen, UK (e-mail: sally.brown@ilt.ac.uk).

Lyn Carson is Lecturer in Applied Politics at the University of Sydney, Australia (e-mail: l.carson@econ.usyd.edu.au).

Helen Edwards is Deputy Director of the Centre for Higher Education Quality at Monash University, Melbourne, Australia (e-mail: helen.edwards@adm.monash.edu.au).

Peter Frederick is Professor of History and American Studies at Wabash College, Crawfordsville, Indiana, USA (e-mail: frederip@Wabash.edu).

Mark D Griffiths is Head of Psychology, Department of Social Sciences, Nottingham Trent University, UK (e-mail: mark.griffiths@ntu.ac.uk).

Brad Haseman is Senior Lecturer in Drama at the Queensland University of Technology, Brisbane, Australia (e-mail: b.haseman@qut.edu.au).

Joy Higgs is Professor in the Faculty of Health Sciences at the University of Sydney, Australia (e-mail: j.higgs@cchs.usyd.edu.au).

Brian Hinton is Lecturer in the School of Data Communications, Queensland University of Technology, Brisbane, Australia (e-mail: b.hinton@qut.edu.au).

Patricia Kalivoda is Assistant Vice President for Academic Affairs (Special Programs) in the University of Georgia, Athens, Georgia, USA (e-mail: tlk@uga.edu).

Peter Knight is Lecturer in Biomedical Sciences at the University of Sydney, Australia (e-mail: p.knight@cchs.usyd.edu.au).

Gary M Lee is Head of the School of Biomedical Sciences at the University of Sydney, Australia (e-mail: G.Lee@cchs.usyd.edu.au).

Bob Lord is Director of Teaching and Learning in the School of Electrical and Computer Engineering at RMIT University, Melbourne, Australia (e-mail: boblord@rmit.edu.au).

Catherine E Manathunga is a lecturer in Teaching and Learning (Higher Education) in the Teaching and Learning Development Unit at the Queensland University of Technology, Brisbane, Australia (e-mail: c.manathunga@qut.edu.au).

Phil Race is a higher education consultant (e-mail: PhilRace@classicfm.net and PhilRace1@classicfm.net).

Brenda Smith is Head of the Generic Centre, Learning and Teaching Support Network, UK (e-mail: Brenda.Smith@ltsn.ac.uk).

Lorraine Stefani is a reader in Academic Practice at the University of Strathclyde, UK (e-mail: L.Stefani@strath.ac.uk).

William M Timpson is Professor, School of Education and Director, The Centre for Learning and Teaching, Colorado State University, USA (e-mail: wtimpson@lamar.colostate.edu).

Graham Webb is Professor and Director, Centre for Higher Education Quality at Monash University, Melbourne, Australia (e-mail: graham.webb@adm.monash.edu.au).

Helen Whiffen is an assistant professor in the Warnell School of Forest Resources at the University of Georgia, Athens, Georgia, USA (e-mail: hwhiffen@smokey.forestry.uga.edu).

Gina Wisker is Director of Learning and Teaching Development, Anglia Polytechnic University, UK (e-mail: G.Wisker@anglia.ac.uk).

Bill G Wright is Associate Professor, Biology, Colorado State University, USA (e-mail: bwright@lamar.colostate.edu).

Stanley Yeo is Professor of Law at Southern Cross University, New South Wales, Australia (e-mail: syeo@scu.edu.au).

INTRODUCTION

WHY A BOOK ON LECTURING?

All of us have memories of hours spent in lectures as students, of good lectures and not so good lectures. Lecturing is the most common form of teaching in higher education and is likely to continue to be used extensively well into the future. Good lecturers inspire us. Their love of the subject and their real concern for students makes spending time in their lectures a joy and an event to be long remembered and cherished. They have a lasting effect on us, on how we view and understand the world. Their professional artistry as teachers, their enthusiasm and their capacity to change and adapt, stimulate us and help us to learn. Equally, many of us have memories of poor lecturers. They left us bored, confused, worried, frustrated and sometimes angry. They may have ruined our interest in a subject. And in between there is the rank and file of day-to-day lecturing that occurs in colleges and universities throughout the world. As lecturers, we spend hundreds of hours delivering and thousands of hours preparing and thinking about lectures. This book is about our experiences.

'Why would you produce a book on lecturing?' was a common reaction when we began putting this volume together. 'Nobody talks about lecturing any more.' True, there is much interest nowadays in areas such as online learning, multimedia, e-learning, problem-based learning, self-directed learning and so on. Yet, the stark reality for most of us and for most of our students is that lecturing is the major teaching and learning method used in universities, and is likely to remain so. This book investigates our reality as lecturers, hopefully, in an interesting, analytical and reflective way.

Typically, as university lecturers, we do *not* tend to talk about our teaching. Our staff room and corridor conversations are rarely about the intricacies and delights of lecturing. This book provides an opportunity for conversations about lecturing. It has been made possible by the openness and bravery of the lecturers who share their stories with us. They have used their own difficulties and adversities to develop their reflective capabilities and to extend the boundaries of what lecturing can be. Their case studies illustrate creativity in dealing with pressures caused by the increasing diversity of the student population and the impact of much larger numbers of students. Additionally, lecturers now face a whole range of external pressures in relation to quality assurance and the need to prepare students for future employment. While such pressures can be a cause of increasing insecurity, the lecturers in this book have used them as opportunities for reflection and for the enhancement of student learning. So in answer to the question 'Why a book on lecturing?' it is our intention to bring to you some interesting cases that present opportunities to consider common issues that arise in lecturing and that will help you to improve your understanding and practice of lecturing.

WHAT DO WE MEAN BY LECTURING?

Traditionally a university lecture was '50–55 minutes of largely uninterrupted discourse from a lecturer with no discussion between students and no student activity other than listening and note-taking' (Gibbs, Habeshaw and Habeshaw, 1992: 9). This is the image that most readily springs to mind when the word lecture is used. This view of lecturing has dominated the architecture of teaching spaces with fixed front podium, tiered seating for large numbers of students and frequently no natural light. It has been reinforced in many cases with the introduction of highly technical lecture theatres where lecturers are further separated from their students by electronic data projection and other devices that tie them to the front of the class.

Lecturing has a well-established place in university teaching particularly at undergraduate level. Lecturers are drawn from all ranks of academics with even the most senior professors undertaking the task. The word lecture is used by administrators to indicate a slot in the timetable where students are taught in a designated space, a lecture theatre, in a group whose size can vary from 20 to 800 and more, and where one lecturer has prime responsibility for 'delivering content'. Because the lecture format can deal with a large number of students using only one lecturer it is often regarded as a 'cheap' form of teaching and thus is attractive in times of decreasing and scarce resources. There is considerable variation in the length of a timetabled lecture, with increasing use being made of times longer than one hour. In one case study in this book, the 'lecture' was timetabled to last for the whole day.

One of the challenges for lecturers in higher education has been to take the traditional 'lecture slot' and turn it into a good learning experience for students. This is in fact how we have approached the definition of lecturing in this book. Cognisant of variations around ideas concerning the lecture and lecturing, we have not attempted a strict definition of the term but instead have viewed it as including a number of parameters, as follows:

- the session has been timetabled as a lecture (as opposed to a seminar or tutorial);
- the expectation is that one lecturer will be responsible for delivery to the whole group, which may have a large number of students;
- the session is face to face or replicates this (eg video of a lecture);
- there are desired learning outcomes for the students.

LECTURING IN THE LITERATURE

There are a number of straightforward and easy-to-read books that give practical information on how to lecture. They represent some of the best-selling and most used books on teaching and learning in higher education. Their contents typically cover setting the context, planning learning outcomes, preparing audiovisual aids, delivery of material, engaging students in active learning, and occasionally discipline in large classes. Usually such publications have the very practical aims of stimulating thought through providing a range of advice and hints and tips that lecturers can readily understand and assimilate into their practice. Examples are Brown and Atkins, 1988; Gibbs, Habeshaw and Habeshaw, 1992; Smith, 1997; Horgan, 1999; McKeachie,1999; Race, 1999 and Newble and Cannon, 2000.

Most provide a solid basis for helping staff structure and deliver lectures and use technology and teaching aids effectively, while more recent additions to the literature emphasize the enhancement of student learning. The continuing popularity of such books illustrates how many staff welcome support for teaching and suggestions for new and different techniques. These books are also popular in staff development courses and are used by a range of staff from graduate teaching assistants to experienced professors because of easy accessibility and jargon-free presentation.

With the development of scholarship and research in higher education an increasing number of books and articles have emerged which seek to explain research findings on how students learn and suggest how those findings can inform appropriate lecturer behaviour. In Europe and Australia, the best known work is based on phenomenographic studies, eg Ramsden, 1992; Marton and Booth 1997; Bowden and Marton, 1998; and Prosser and Trigwell, 1998. In North America, there has been more emphasis on using a cognitive psychology approach to understanding how students learn, eg McKeachie, 1999. The advent of new technologies has resulted in volumes that encourage lecturers to rethink some of their teaching approaches, eg Laurillard, 1994; Maier and Warren, 2000.

All these authors take understanding of how students learn as their central focus and consider how research results can be used to inform teaching. *Teaching for Quality Learning at University* (Biggs, 1999) is a particularly good example of integrating a research focus with hands-on practical strategies. In his preface Biggs states 'This book is intended to help university teachers reflect on and improve the quality of their teaching, despite the conditions of class size and student diversity that seem to make good teaching more difficult than ever' (Biggs, 1999: xi). Throughout the book, he advocates the deceptively simple message of aligning objectives, teaching methods and assessment tasks in a process he calls 'constructive alignment'.

All these texts have in common a focus on understanding, active student involvement in learning and constructing meaning. The traditional lecture method is not perceived as being a particularly good method for achieving such pedagogic aims. McKeachie (1999) cites a long list of studies that show that the lecture is as effective as any other method in conveying factual knowledge but that on other criteria such as attitude change, development of thinking and problem solving, the lecture falls short of more student-active methods. Yet, as we have remarked, the lecture is by far the most common teaching method in higher education. Given that we are unlikely to change that reality, at least in the medium term, the question might then be asked, how can lecturing be used to encourage active student learning and the construction of meaning? Some of the case studies in this book illustrate just how lecturers came to realize the importance of a student learning focus in lecturing and adapted their practice accordingly. The authors of the case studies demonstrate many ways in which the traditional lecture can be transformed into an active and enjoyable learning experience for students and staff. The authors' reflections on their experiences demonstrate for us a variety of creative ways to bring together hints and tips, active student learning, and reflective practice into the lecturing format.

THE CASES

We have taken a wide-ranging approach to the inclusion of cases in this book. Our cases range from a one-hour slot to a six-hour slot; and from a one-off visiting lecture to a semester-length course. We have deliberately included cases where much of the teaching and learning activity is quite different from the teacher-focused information delivery traditionally associated with lectures. We have done this because we would like to see the reality of lecturing in higher education shift from an information-delivery model to a student-learning model. With such a shift comes the need to adapt traditional methods of teaching and to vary the mixture of teaching and learning activities that occur within 'a lecture'. We need to focus on the purpose and effectiveness of this mixture of activities in order to ensure good learning experiences for students. Universities still expect staff to lecture. There has never been so much use made of lectures, nor have there been so many exciting teaching and learning episodes happening within the timetable slot of 'lecture'. This book explores 17 such episodes as case studies.

The journey of a person developing as a university teacher is typically not a linear one. Teachers do not start at 'the beginning' and proceed across time to some defined end. Rather a teacher's journey is constantly changing. It changes with external factors such as the subjects, courses and programmes taught, class size and year level, increasing student diversity and the university in which the teacher is working. It changes with internal factors such as the teacher's journey of self-knowledge and reflection, often in terms of a stronger focus on student learning and a deepening understanding that students construct knowledge and that each student reacts differently to content and the process of teaching. It changes as teachers feel the desire to try new and different approaches. It changes when internal or external funding facilitates project work, where teams of staff and students can share and develop new ideas. It changes with the support available within the institution and whether the climate is supportive of disseminating effective practice. Such a journey is a process of continuing professional development, of reflection on action and reflection in action (Schön, 1987). The case studies in this book were chosen to provide examples from lecturers at many points on that journey of continuing professional development.

The cases are written by 21 faculty members from Australia, the UK and North America. They come from a range of disciplines and backgrounds including American studies, biology, biomedical sciences, data communication, drama, education, education development, engineering, English, forestry, history, information technology, law, learning and teaching support, politics, physiotherapy, psychology, and radiography. Contributors were invited to tell their story of a critical incident that had actually happened to them as lecturers, and which led to them learning and growing in their journey as lecturers. Again, each case tells a real story based on an actual situation and its resolution.

As with all books in this series, each case is preceded by an indication of the main issue or issues raised, and by brief background information to set the context for the 'action'. The case proper consists of two or more parts, each concluding with a few questions for you to consider. We have introduced this reflective break between parts of a case at a point where an action must be taken and/or a decision made. You are invited to step into the writer's shoes at this point and decide not only what you think should be done next but also what you think will actually happen next given the circumstances of the case. After discovering what actually did happen, you will be asked to reflect on how the situation was handled and to consider some of the questions and issues raised by the case. At the end, there is a case reporter's discussion that raises questions such as:

- How well was the situation handled?
- What other options might there have been for dealing with it?
- What lessons did the reporter and his or her colleagues learn from the experience?
- What lessons are there for others from the case?

The discussions are by no means exhaustive in that other important issues and/or questions could be examined, and you may well identify issues or perspectives that have not been mentioned. We sought to strike a balance between leaving each situation equivocal and open to individual interpretation on the one hand and tightly defining issues and providing guidance on the other. Nor is the discussion intended to give 'the right answer' to a problem. We do not believe that there is a simple and unequivocal 'right answer' in cases such as these, although, under the circumstances described, some solutions may be better than others. The purpose of the discussion is to explore the issues raised and to encourage you to make your own decisions based upon your interpretation of and reflections on the case. The intent is that you may then apply the insights gained from this experience as you deal with similar situations in your own lecturing.

The book concludes with a brief list of suggested readings on lecturing. Most of the readings are of general applicability rather than being directed towards specific issues or events discussed in the cases. The reading list is intended to be broad and immediately useful, rather than comprehensive. The editors and contributors would welcome enquiries from readers who would like more information. Electronic mail addresses are given for the editors and case reporters.

ISSUES IN LECTURING

A number of issues about lecturing emerge from the case studies presented here and most university lecturers will face at least some of these situations in their teaching.

There are organizational and structural issues. With the rise in student numbers and the decreasing unit of resource, more use is made of service teaching and the 'one-off' lecture. This presents particular challenges for both staff and students and raises a number of questions in relation to the ongoing support needed for all staff as part of professional development. There has also been increasing pressure from employers to ensure students acquire 'generic' graduate attributes, such as problem-solving skills, skills of critical analysis, communication skills, etc. A number of the case studies focus on these issues.

To cope with increasing numbers of students universities continue to build larger and more highly technical lecture theatres and in many cases with fixed tiered seating. This can create greater space barriers between lecturer and students as data protection and video conferencing equipment begin to fill the space between lecturer and student. In their turn increased numbers have highlighted the problem of disruptive students. How do you deal with frequent interruptions caused by mobile phones going off or even two students in a passionate embrace?

Other case studies highlight issues around the process of teaching. With the increasing emphasis on student learning in lectures, a number of cases illustrate creative strategies to engage students actively and meaningfully in their learning. This can lead to problems when dealing with controversial topics and sensitive issues. Do you avoid these issues or confront them 'head on'? As lecturers experiment with new ideas and techniques, strategies are required for coping with the unexpected. What do you do when something goes drastically wrong?

With the increasing pressure for accountability, how do you evaluate your teaching? How do you record, value and learn from your experiences – the scholarship of teaching? Indeed, how do you know if you are successful in a lecture, in a course of lectures, as a lecturer, as a professional? A number of the case studies give very honest and often painful accounts of how lecturers listened and reacted to student feedback and as a result adopted a reflective approach to their teaching. A number of success stories demonstrate how a climate of trust and support from colleagues led to enhanced student learning and increased lecturer satisfaction.

However, perhaps the most potent issues are around the affective and emotional side of being a lecturer in higher education. The cases illustrate the acutely lonely task of preparing and delivering a lecture programme and the complexity of what is expected of lecturers. There are increasing pressures to 'perform' in the lecture and be flexible, leading to the need for 'on the spot' reacting, thinking and adjusting. How would you turn adverse moments into positive experiences and action through reflection? Finally, with all the many changes that occur how do you acquire the tenacity to continue when you are physically and mentally exhausted.

These are only some of the many rich areas for thought and action about lecturing raised in the case studies. What these areas do highlight is the diverse and multifaceted role of the lecturer. Just as we think we have got to grips with one issue, a different one comes along.

HOW TO USE THIS BOOK

We recommend that, as you read a case, you 'play the game' and read only Part 1, before reflecting and noting your impressions of what is going on, what courses of action could be taken next, what you think will happen next and what course of action you would pursue. The same applies to Part 2 (and others, where relevant). Questions have been provided at the end of each part of a case to assist you in framing your interpretation of and response to what is happening. In many instances, the questions are specific to the case, but some general questions that would be appropriate for most cases include the following.

At the end of Part 1, ask:

- What is going on here?
- What factors may have contributed to the situation described?
- How does the case reporter appear to see the situation?
- What other interpretations might there be?
- How might the situation be handled?
- What sorts of consequences might be expected from the possible actions?
- Given the nature of the participants, how will the situation probably be dealt with?

After the final part and the discussion, ask:

- How well was the situation handled?
- What general issues are brought out by the case?
- What do the case and its issues mean for you, the reader?

We believe that as an individual reader you will derive valuable insights if you use the case studies and discussions in this way. However, we suggest that you will also find it valuable to meet with colleagues to share impressions of the cases and insights obtained from them. The cases can serve as resources for advanced training and development of teaching staff and administrators. In fact, the cases presented in a previous book (Schwartz and Webb, 1993) were both the products of and the discussion materials for a series of group discussions in a faculty development programme. Others have also described the use of case studies in faculty development for teachers (Christensen, 1987; Hutchings, 1993; Wilkerson and Boehrer, 1992).

Whether done formally or informally, consideration of the cases and issues by groups of colleagues has benefits beyond those that may be obtained from individual reading. In discussions with colleagues, lecturers can confront their own perceptions and readings of cases, and face the possibility that their interpretations may not be shared by others. Justifying these interpretations can bring teachers face to face with their philosophies of human nature and the nature of education. This can serve to stimulate them to become more reflective about their own practices. They may be challenged to come to terms with alternative conceptions and interpretations of each case. Teachers may be stimulated to re-examine and re-evaluate some of the central features of their own views by seeking to understand one another's interpretations and experiences and the outlooks that shape them. The discussion sections in this book may provide a starting point, but there are further opportunities for quality discussion between colleagues on these issues.

Reflection in teaching is crucial regardless of whether you read the cases as an individual or discuss them with colleagues. It is from this effort that teachers are likely to obtain the most benefit from the cases (Harden *et al*, 1999; Fincher *et al*, 2000). Interestingly, the case writers themselves, in developing the cases for this book, discovered the value of reflecting on the educational experiences they reported. The authors of the case studies in this book had the courage to discuss some critical experiences as lecturers openly. In doing so they have identified issues that you can continue to reflect on and explore, since there are clearly no quick fixes to the issues raised.

We trust that your own reflection on lecturing and on the issues raised by the cases presented in this book will be useful and will stimulate you to try new approaches in your own lecturing in order to enhance student learning. We wish you every success with your students.

REFERENCES

Biggs, J (1999) *Teaching for Quality Learning at University*, Society for Research into Higher Education and Open University Press, Buckingham

Bowden, J and Marton, F (1998) *The University of Learning: Beyond quality and competence in higher education*, Kogan Page, London

Brown, G and Atkins, M (1988) *Effective Teaching in Higher Education*, Methuen, London

Christensen, C R (1987) *Teaching and the Case Method*, Harvard Business School, Boston

Fincher, R M *et al* (2000) Scholarship in teaching: An imperative for the 21st century, *Academic Medicine*, **75**, pp 887–94

Gibbs, G; Habeshaw, S and Habeshaw, T (1992) *53 Interesting Things to Do in Your Lectures*, Technical and Educational Services, Bristol

Harden, R M *et al* (1999) BEME Guide No 1: Best evidence medical education, *Medical Teacher*, **21**, pp 553–62

Horgan, J (1999) Lecturing for Learning, in *A Handbook for Teaching and Learning in Higher Education*, ed S Marshall, H Fry and S Ketteridge, pp 83–94, Kogan Page, London

Hutchings, P (1993) *Using Cases to Improve College Teaching: A guide to more reflective practice*, American Association for Higher Education, Washington, DC

Laurillard, D (1994) *Rethinking University Teaching: A framework for the effective use of educational technology*, Routledge, London

Maier, P and Warren, A (2000) *Integrating Technology in Learning and Teaching: A practical guide for educators*, Kogan Page, London

Marton, F and Booth, S A (1997) *Learning and Awareness*, Lawrence Erlbaum, Hillsdale, New Jersey

McKeachie, W J (1999) *McKeachie's Teaching Tips, Strategies, Research, and Theory for College and University Teachers*, 10th edn, Houghton Mifflin Company, New York

Newble, D and Cannon, R (2000) *A Handbook for Teachers in Universities and Colleges*, Kogan Page, London

Prosser, M and Trigwell, K (1998) *Understanding Learning and Teaching*, Open University Press, Buckingham

Race, P (ed) (1999) *2000 Tips for Lecturers*, Kogan Page, London

Ramsden, P (1992) *Learning to Teach in Higher Education*, Routledge, London

Schön, D (1987) *Educating the Reflective Practitioner*, Jossey-Bass, New York

Schwartz, P and Webb, G (1993) *Case Studies on Teaching in Higher Education*, Kogan Page, London

Smith, B (1997) *Lecturing to Large Groups*, SEDA, Birmingham

Wilkerson, L and Boehrer, J (1992) Using cases about teaching for faculty development, *To Improve the Academy*, **11**, pp 253–62

KEY COMPETENCIES IN LECTURING

CHAPTER 1

LEARNING FROM OBJECTIVES

Case reporter: Stanley Yeo

ISSUES RAISED

The issues raised by this case focus on the pressures faced by a more junior lecturer taking over a well-established lecture course that has been taken for many years by a senior academic. The particular issue concerns a new lecturer introducing changes to a course without feeling able to modify the already well-established course structure significantly. The issue for students is that they are pulled in the direction of both the old and the new.

BACKGROUND

This case occurred in a large compulsory second-year criminal law class in an Australian university. A 33-year-old male lecturer who had three years of lecturing experience had just taken sole responsibility for lecturing the course. In the previous year, he had assisted a well-respected senior academic who had been teaching the course for six years. The students were mainly in their early 20s.

PART 1

I was excited at the prospect of implementing some new ideas and improvements when I 'inherited' the second-year criminal law course. My predecessor on the course, Dr Arnold, a respected senior academic, had closely followed the coverage, style and approach of a conventional, well-regarded and frequently prescribed textbook on criminal law. The course content complied with the Faculty's policy of covering all the topics identified by the Board of Legal Practitioners as being essential for practice. Students were informed that the primary objective of the course was 'to provide students with a basic understanding of the general principles of criminal responsibility through a study of major crimes and defences'.

In my first year of taking over the course, I felt constrained to carry on in much the same way that Dr Arnold had taught the course. This feeling of constraint stemmed from:

- deference to my predecessor;
- a lack of confidence to introduce changes in my initial year of taking full responsibility for teaching the course;
- pressure of time.

While these forces weighed heavily, I still wanted to add my own mark to the course. I therefore decided to add two further objectives to the primary objective of providing students with a basic understanding of the general principles of criminal responsibility. My additional objectives were:

- to develop the students' skills of critical appraisal of social institutions, and community values and expectations in relation to criminal behaviour;
- to encourage students to think about the ways in which power structures in society are reproduced by the criminal law and justice system.

These new objectives reflected a critical legal studies approach. In this approach, conventional paradigms and assumptions on which the law is based are challenged, resulting in new ways of thinking about the law.

Thrilled by my changes to the course, I commenced compiling a set of supplementary reading materials that were chosen to raise student awareness and appreciation of these additional objectives. The set comprised articles on a few selected topics that were covered by the course. For example, one of the selected articles was by Alison Young on the crime of rape and was entitled 'The Waste Land of the Law, The Wordless Song of the Rape Victim'. The conventional treatment of this topic in a criminal law course is to identify the elements of the crime of rape that the prosecution has to prove to secure a conviction. Young's article goes well beyond such treatment by explaining the way the criminal trial proceedings greatly undermine the female rape victim's narrative of the alleged crime so as to work in favour of the male defendant. Students were required to purchase both the standard textbook on criminal law and the supplementary reading materials.

The class comprised 110 students and met twice a week for one-hour lectures and once a fortnight for one-hour tutorials. The students were a mix of fresh school leavers and mature-age students and about equal in terms of gender distribution. The course information booklet contained a reading list of materials which students were encouraged to digest in advance of the lectures. The list referred students to the relevant pages in the prescribed textbook for each topic covered in the course. Whenever the opportunity arose, the reading list also referred students to articles in the set of supplementary reading materials that dealt with a specific topic. At the first lecture, I went through the course objectives with the students, explaining the importance of each objective to their understanding of the practice and ongoing development of the criminal law.

My lectures usually took the form of presenting a topic in much the same way as my predecessor had done. This involved informing students of the requirements of the law, referring them to the leading cases and statutory provisions governing the topic, and highlighting issues of contention or uncertainty in the law. In the course of each lecture, I would periodically refer students to the prescribed textbook for further elucidation of a particular issue.

As the term progressed, I frequently found myself hard pressed for time trying to complete all I wanted to say at the lectures. When I came to lecture a topic which required students to read something from the supplementary reading material, I often found that all that I could manage, given the limited lecture time available, was to summarize what the article said briefly and to invite students to read it for themselves alongside the conventional treatment of the topic in the prescribed textbook. I intensely disliked doing this, and realized that I was requiring my students to digest conceptually difficult and often challenging material with very little guidance from me.

One rainy wintry morning, about a third of the way through the term and midway through a lecture, a student called Fiona interjected with the question: 'But wouldn't the outcome be different if the criminal law were to recognize the narrative of the female complainant?' This question was clearly critical of certain assumptions in criminal law concerning the behaviour of a female crime victim and the way her behaviour might be viewed by the male defendant. I knew by her question that Fiona had read and digested the previously mentioned article by Alison Young and was seeking to apply the lessons learnt from that article to the present topic. I realized unhappily that I had a decision on my hands. Since I had not included an article in the supplementary material on this particular topic, I was reluctant to engage in any discussion with Fiona. Furthermore, the minutes were fast ticking away and I still had some remaining issues that I wanted to cover in the ten minutes left before the end of the lecture.

I acknowledged to Fiona that hers was a good question that might more usefully be taken up at tutorials. Fiona replied by saying, 'There's already far too much that needs to be covered during the tutorials. I'm really fed up at being encouraged on the one hand to "think critically" in respect of one area of the law but dissuaded from doing so in another area.' At this juncture, Amy, another student, interjected saying, 'I'm quite happy with this situation and as far as I'm concerned, the approach to criminal law in our prescribed textbook is what is required for legal practice and I can take or leave all this critical legal studies bullshit. Anyway, it's bound to appear as an option question in the exam that I can afford to leave out.' Bill, a third student, then yelled out in agreement, saying that he was already having difficulty keeping up with the reading of the prescribed text and the course could have done without the supplementary set of materials. Fiona then pointedly challenged me to say whether my occasional brief reference to those materials was mere tokenism towards critical legal studies.

- What do you think were the main factors leading to this situation?
- What would you have done if confronted with this situation?
- What do you think the lecturer's reply was to this challenge?
- What actions could the lecturer take after the class?
- What do you think the lecturer actually did subsequently?

PART 2

After a minute's reflection, I decided to face the challenge head on by sharing my own frustrations with the class and did so with a feeling of liberation and empowerment. I told the class that the issue raised by Fiona was a very real concern that had been bothering me for some time. I stood by my inclusion of the additional course objectives and supplementary materials and I reiterated my reasons for including them as part of the course.

I admitted to the class that I had not clearly translated the new objectives into my lecture presentations and my selection of prescribed readings. This failure had caused students to have differing views about the relative importance of the new objectives. I also acknowledged to the students that I might have caused them to be unclear over what I was expecting from them when evaluating their performance at the examination.

In the closing minutes of the lecture I assured the class that 'I'll clarify my position at the next lecture and will take firm measures to remove any misunderstandings or misconceptions about the course objectives and what I expect of you in achieving those objectives.' It was with a deep sense of resolve that I left the lecture theatre that rainy wintry morning.

I proceeded immediately to Dr Arnold's office and was relieved to find him there. Over a mug of hot chocolate, I sought his advice on what could be done. To achieve a greater balance of views and ideas, I also spoke at length with a lecturer from the Law Faculty of another university who was well known for teaching her criminal law course wholly from a critical legal studies perspective. From both discussions, I received much empathy, encouragement and support.

In particular, my self-confidence was boosted. I was assured that my own set of course objectives was as good as any other set and that there is no single preferred way of teaching criminal law. On reflection, I learnt that what was vital for good teaching was to be crystal clear about the way I intended to meet those course objectives through my lectures and tutorials, the prescribed reading materials and the methods of assessment. To discharge my teaching duties well, I needed to provide students with full and precise details of the subject matters that they would be learning in the course, what they could expect from me as their teacher and what I expected of them in return. Further, I needed to identify the salient features of my course that I hoped would make it a specially beneficial and enjoyable one.

Since there were still another eight weeks left of the course I knew that, with some adjustment and forward planning, I could teach it without needing to abandon my two new course objectives. I went carefully through the remaining lecture topics for the course and deliberated upon which course objective(s) were ideally suited to be covered by each of those topics. In doing so, I was taking the stance that I should be guided by which topic might be best suited to meeting a particular course objective. I was content to accept that this meant that I would not be able to cover all the topics one might normally expect of a criminal law course. This led to my implementing several measures for the remainder of the course.

First, I sought to discover whether any of the topics covered by the course that I had inherited could be safely removed. I started by identifying all the topics that the Board of Legal Practitioners required us to deal with. I found that there were two topics that could be taken out, and I did so. Doing this took some pressure off me.

Next, I went carefully through each topic covered by my course to determine which course objective(s) could be met by that topic. After my initial run through of this exercise, I found that one or two objectives were being met much more frequently than others. Additionally, I noted that my intended coverage of several forthcoming topics merely reinforced what my students already knew about a specific rule of criminal law. Thereafter, I sought to avoid this imbalance and repetition by thinking of alternative ways of presenting a particular topic that would satisfy a less well-served objective rather than a frequently served one. I achieved all of this with a deep sense of satisfaction and relief.

My third strategy was to revise my prescribed reading list. I became much more selective about the materials that I was requiring the students to read, conscious of the student complaint of being overloaded with reading materials. I imposed on myself the rule of thumb that students should be required to read a maximum of 30 printed pages for each one-hour lecture. This was as much reading material as I could expect students to digest in the three-hour pre-lecture preparation time prescribed for the course. A significant outcome of this measure was that I freed students of the need to refer to the prescribed textbook for each topic covered by the course. Instead, they were required to read the articles in the supplementary reading materials.

My fourth measure had the positive consequences of making my class preparation both easier and more enjoyable. I distributed handouts that informed students of both the objectives of the particular lecture and of the lecture outline. I found that the preparation of these handouts made me much more focused as to how I should plan my lecture to meet its stated objectives and also, more generally, the objectives of the course. In planning my lecture, I took pains to ensure that it would adhere closely to the prescribed reading materials for the particular topic. In this way, students were clearly informed of what exactly I was seeking to achieve when lecturing on a specific topic and this was confirmed for them when they came to reading the prescribed materials. This practice regularly declared to my students that I wanted to provide them with a sampling of different approaches to the criminal law rather than presenting them with a single approach. Additionally, it declared to them my intention of applying only certain approaches to selected topics rather than having all the approaches applied to each topic.

Fifthly, in line with the preceding measures, I reworked the set of tutorial problems so that they directly correlated with my lecture presentation and the selection of prescribed materials.

Finally, I went about drafting two sets of examination papers containing a spread of questions to test students' comprehension of the lectures and prescribed reading materials. I distributed the first set to my students at the next lecture, announcing that I would discuss it with them at the final lecture as a trial run. I kept the second set for use at the examination proper. The students listened attentively as I outlined these measures. The remainder of the lecture went smoothly with sufficient time left for me to cover the content planned for that lecture and to answer some questions raised by the students.

Having implemented these measures, I felt confident that I would be able to achieve all my course objectives in the remaining weeks without imposing undue demands on the students. My confidence was fully affirmed when, within a space of two weeks, Fiona and Bill told me of their own accord that they were very pleased with my measures that had enabled them really to enjoy the study of criminal law. Amy did not come forward in the same way, but neither did she protest any further during the remainder of the course.

- How do you think the lecturer handled the situation?
- If faced with a similar situation, how would you have acted?
- What would you have done differently?

DISCUSSION

A lecturer 'inheriting' another's course is an all too common occurrence. So too is the tendency for the predecessor to be a more senior or experienced teacher of the course, and for the new lecturer to be given very little time to prepare for taking over the course. In these circumstances, the lecturer's introduction of new objectives and materials to the course was courageous and admirable.

However, as might be expected, the lecturer's hurried and rather piecemeal changes to the course were bound to attract the kind of problems revealed in this case as:

- the lecturer found himself hard pressed to cover all the material in lectures;
- students had differing ideas about what the course objectives were and what was expected of them when approaching a particular topic;
- students were suffering from an overload of prescribed reading materials;
- students were uncertain about how the critical legal studies component would be assessed in the examination;
- the tutorials were not being efficiently utilized as a forum in which students could confirm or clarify their understanding of the lectures and reading materials.

The measures taken by the lecturer after the critical event solved or at least reduced these problems. The common denominator of all these measures was the close and consistent adherence to the stated course objectives in classes (both lectures and tutorials) as well as in the examination paper. Henceforth, both the lecturer and the students were very clear about what the course objectives were, and could readily match the course content and assessment with those objectives. Drawing upon analogy, only from that point on did the lecturer actually move from being first officer to the captain of the ship. He became clear where he wanted the ship to go and the tasks it would perform, he charted the maps and showed them to his crew members, and he provided them with relevant written manuals and conducted regular drills to keep them alert and fit for the tasks that lay ahead. And throughout all of this, he maintained the speed of his ship at a steady and not overly demanding pace.

Since the lecturer had to do some fast thinking and take quick action part way through the course, it was only to be expected that there would be much room for improvement. This was reflected in the lecturer's student evaluation results at the end of the term, compared with the following year when he had more time for reflection and preparation before teaching the course again. Sixty-five per cent of respondents said that the lecturer made clear 'all the time' what they needed to do to be successful in the course compared to 86 per cent in the following year.

One of the problems that the lecturer could not resolve to his entire satisfaction was the selection of prescribed texts and materials. The easiest route was to prescribe a standard text and follow it closely as his predecessor had done. However, since he wanted his course to involve a mixture of conventional and critical approaches to criminal law, he had difficulty finding a single appropriate text to prescribe. Bearing in mind the high cost of legal texts, the lecturer in ensuing years abandoned prescribing the conventional criminal law text relied on by his predecessor. In its place, he compiled his own set of readings which involved much more work for him but which he believed to be worthwhile because this gave him more control over the reading materials and their use in his course.

What might be learnt from this is that, in making course objectives paramount, lecturers must be prepared to develop their own set of reading materials to complement those objectives. While this invariably involves a fair amount of extra work, it can be a most rewarding exercise for the lecturer and may even provide the opportunity for publishing a textbook of his or her own.

In conclusion, it occurred to the lecturer as a result of this experience that the key to good lecturing is really simple – teach only what is really necessary to achieve your course objectives and be sure to align course content and assessment with those objectives.

CHAPTER 2

NEW AT THIS

Case reporter: Sally Brown

ISSUES RAISED

This case raises the issue of an inexperienced and untrained lecturer dealing with disruptive students.

BACKGROUND

The case occurred at a large northern metropolitan university in the UK. A recently appointed female has been asked to undertake a series of lectures on a first-year communication course for 120 engineering students. Around 20 per cent of these students come from outside the UK.

PART 1

I now had to give my first lecture to the whole cohort of first-year students. I felt rather nervous as I entered the lecture room on the first morning of the lecture series. I was faced with a sea of students' faces, most of them male. I was still new to teaching and therefore any new context still caused me a certain amount of anxiety.

As part of a team, I had provided a series of seminars to support the development of students' key skills including such topics as study skills, effective report writing, giving presentations, taking part in and chairing meetings and preparation for employment (letters of application, CVs and interviews). I enjoyed giving these seminars. We had collectively devised a range of practical activities for the students. All of the materials and activities were directly relevant to students' needs at the time and for future student placements and employment. I felt well prepared for these seminars and materials to support the activities were piled high on my office desk. However, by comparison, preparing the lectures made me lose some sleep.

The first few weeks seemed to go reasonably well. My preparation work paid off as I felt on top of my subject and I was reasonably pleased with the way my voice projected in a room with quite a difficult acoustic. I had put some time into mastering PowerPoint and had learned quite a few of the little tricks. However, five weeks in, I started to get really rattled by the amount of disruptive behaviour that was going on in my lectures.

There were often students arriving up to ten minutes late and disrupting other students as they arrived. The tiered seating arrangement in the lecture room made it impossible for latecomers to slip into the back rows as the entry door was at the front of the room, beside the demonstration desk. Furthermore, the seating was designed to be able to be collapsed to the back of the room at exam times so that exam desks could be set out on the floor, so it was noisy whenever people walked up the steps. The noise really put me off my stroke, but when I remonstrated, they all had perfectly good excuses. One of the very few women students, Jan, was one of the worst offenders, but then I found out she was doing a three-mile round journey by bus to the child minder's every morning to drop off her toddler, and the buses were notorious for their unreliability.

Another problem that I found rather upsetting was that despite my pleas, some students, particularly those from outside the UK were chatting to one another all the way through the lectures. I found this both disturbing to my concentration and rather discourteous. I tried to suppress the babble, by being firm and by appealing to their better natures, but it continued nevertheless.

I felt undermined, and the worse the students behaviour became, the more flustered I felt, which in turn seemed to make them worse yet. The crunch came one day after I had decided to ignore the mobile phones going off, Ali listening to a cricket commentary on a headset while the lecture was in progress, Simeon discreetly but obviously doing a crossword from the newspaper, and even Mike, who was so good in the seminars, snoozing quietly. The last straw was when I noticed Liz in a passionate embrace with Paul in the back row, as if this was a cinema rather than a lecture theatre and first thing in the morning too! I was so surprised by this that I stopped mid-sentence and stared, as did all the other students until at last the passionate couple came up for air and found 59 pairs of eyes looking at them! As I left the lecture theatre it occurred to me that I was now dreading lectures and that perhaps I should even begin to think about changing jobs.

- Why do you think the students were behaving in this way?
- What would you do in this situation?

PART 2

On calming down again, I decided to make my first call the member of staff responsible for room timetabling. I tried my hardest to get a different room to teach in, with fixed seating that would not be so noisy when people arrived late, but despite all my cajoling and pleading, this proved impossible. I tried to negotiate having the temporary seating pushed back permanently and the exam desks used at all times, but this proved neither popular with my colleagues nor practical to implement, as the room held far fewer students sitting at exam desks than in the tiered seating.

My attempts to exhort students to arrive promptly were unsuccessful, as a handful of students continued to arrive late and with plausible reasons or excuses. One old hand in the department advised locking the door at five minutes past the hour (contravening fire regulations) or only giving handouts to those who arrived on time, but both of these solutions seemed rather draconian and not in accord with my personal style of teaching and the relationship I wanted to develop with the students. My pragmatic but not entirely successful solution was to insist that early arrivals filled up the seats at the back of the room, leaving the front row empty for latecomers. This was not terribly popular with those students who came on time and did not like to be directed where to sit, but it did at least mean that disruption was minimized and I kept my cool.

I also decided to consult an older colleague, Marcia, who had been working on the team with similar groups of students for a number of years. Marcia, a tremendous support in times of trial, helped to throw some light on the chattering international students. She suggested that at least some of them might be translating for one another, and that, rather than being a nuisance, they were actually doing their best to help less fluent classmates follow what I was saying. She advised that I should use handouts that provided far more key words and information than I had been used to giving and also suggested providing more detailed information as back up on my Web page.

At the next lecture, I told students generally about my new strategy. I suggested that students whose first language was not English spend more time listening and making sense of what I was saying, and less time struggling to write down everything I said. As a result, the level of babble reduced somewhat, although it did not completely disappear. However, as I now recognized what was going on, I did not find it nearly so annoying. In fact, a high level of background noise cued me to be particularly careful with words I thought the international students might be finding difficult.

The discourteous individuals were more difficult to deal with. A colleague in another department suggested a one-off strategy to cope with the mobile phone users. This colleague had started his lecture by saying how fed up he was with phones ringing in class. He told all students to turn off their phones as they entered the room and he warned them that he would confiscate and destroy the next ringing phone in his lecture. True to his word, the next time a phone rang, he marched up to the student, collected the phone, took it down to the front of the room and produced a hammer. Before the horrified eyes of the owner, he proceeded to smash away and throw the remnants in the bin. He then continued lecturing but at the end of the lecture returned the student's undamaged mobile with a warning not to let it happen again. He had of course swapped the original for a non-functioning phone he had brought in from home. Dramatic as it was, I decided this was not the approach for me.

Instead I took advice from a colleague in the Educational Development Unit (following Marcia's suggestion to go and look them up), who proposed tackling the issue on two fronts. First I used ten minutes at the beginning of the next lecture to talk to the students about the issue. They told me all about their transport difficulties, early starts, the conflicting pressures of studying and having to work to earn money, sheer exhaustion and the competing demands of Student Night at the local nightclub.

I told them how disconcerting I found their alternative activities in the classroom and about the pressures of time on curriculum delivery and my desire to be professional in my job. As a result, we came up with a mutually agreed set of ground rules which established that behaviours which were disruptive to other students or to me were to be outlawed, while those which were ill-mannered but harmless (like sleeping) were to be ignored. (In fact, I found out that Mike, who had so blatantly slept through my last lecture, had spent the night before at the hospital with his sick wife.) There were university regulations on matters like eating and drinking in lecture rooms and about the use of mobile phones, and I made it clear that I expected students to conform to these. The result was some immediate improvement in behaviour overall, which gradually tailed off a little as students lapsed from their good intentions. Nevertheless, I felt I had made some progress and students in the class became more involved in monitoring the behaviour of others.

My other strategy, following advice from the Educational Development Unit, was to rethink my lecturing technique. I started to commence each lecture with a slide showing what they should expect to get out of the lecture and how this session fitted in with the module as a whole. Helping the students to understand the links between the overview lectures and the associated seminars seemed to help them recognize the importance of the lecture content. I experimented with ways of breaking up the lecture sessions with small activities in which it was expected that students would confer with one another. This meant that they were less likely to talk through the presentation sections of my lecture. By asking students to work on small tasks, I also found that they were less likely to lose concentration and therefore be disruptive. I tried to ensure that the presentation elements never lasted more than 15 minutes or so without some element of activity, questions or visual stimuli. This made it more difficult to get through the material, but it seemed to help to make the process more active for the students and less stressful for me.

I also decided to limit my use of PowerPoint presentations so as to avoid 'death by bullet point' and from time to time I spoke directly without slides, especially when providing an overview of the key topics. I made it clear to students when I expected them to write down what was being said, when they should follow the relevant sections in the handouts and when they should just listen and think. I also made use of short trigger extracts of videos of people being interviewed and in meetings, with associated follow-up tasks for the students. This took more organization in terms of having the equipment set up and the tapes wound to just the right point, but added a sense of immediacy to the topics that had been lacking before.

- How well do you think the teacher handled the situation?
- What else could she have done?
- Have you ever faced a similar situation and if so, how did you handle it?

DISCUSSION

I did not find the changes I made caused my problems to disappear overnight. Some students continued to behave badly in my lectures, but I found the distractions less upsetting than I had done previously. I negotiated with the course team to reduce the total number of lectures being given, as the work undertaken by students in seminars seemed to me to be far more productive, given the subject matter. However, it was difficult with me being the new member of the team to go in and tell my more experienced colleagues to stop doing what they have been doing for years.

I also developed a topic handbook for the module with concrete examples and written guidance that I would like ultimately to use to replace some elements of the lectures. I am feeling a lot better about it now, and learning to accept that the rapt audiences of students you see in the movies are not the way things are for most of us lesser mortals. I now find it easier to address unacceptable behaviour without getting angry as I once did, although I sometimes find myself reminding students of the ground rules between gritted teeth. It helped a lot to talk to the students and recognize the problems some of them were facing in getting in to classes on time, when they are carrying heavy domestic responsibilities and unavoidable paid employment.

I came to recognize something that probably seems like old hat to more experienced colleagues: that there is not a single right way to give lectures or respond to student behaviour. Talking to the colleagues who advised me also made me realize that what is important is to find an approach that suits the individual and that one can comfortably work with. I also came to understand that this is not a thing that can just be fixed overnight. Students can find countless ways to disrupt lectures, some intentional and some not, and being able to cope with what the situation throws up is all part of developing the confidence one needs to be a lecturer. It is also a great help to know that there are other people who can help, who have been through equally annoying and distressing experiences, and that having disruptive students in a class is not necessarily a reflection on the lecturer, but can be just a fact of life.

My experience raises a number of issues that apply generally to many staff in universities. In particular, it raises questions about the kinds of support those new to the role of lecturer can expect in the early stages of their career. I was unfortunate in that, having started my contract with the university half way through the academic year, I had not been able to join the programme for new lecturers that the university required all untrained staff to undertake in their first year of teaching.

Therefore, I was thrown in at the deep end, under the assumption that, as a bright and capable person, I would be able to pick up the skills I needed as I went along. I was not even able to attend the one-day teaching orientation course that the university offered at the start of every term to new staff, which gave basic guidance on teaching methodologies, as this had clashed with my first day of lecturing. I had not had time to find my way to the excellent Learning and Teaching Resource Centre where there were lots of useful introductory handbooks and guides giving practical advice on starting out as a lecturer. Therefore, the only thing I had to base my approach to lecturing on was my own rather patchy experience of being lectured to as a student. Some of the more idiosyncratic advice of colleagues helped to lighten the more desperate moments, but provided little by way of practical guidance. On the other hand, advice from colleagues to seek further help proved critical.

With ever-closer external scrutiny of the student learning experience by external agencies such as the Quality Assurance Agency (QAA) in the UK and with students becoming ever more litigious if they feel that failure can be ascribed to weak teaching, the development of teaching skills for new lecturers is of real concern. Many universities now offer programmes for new staff to prepare them for the full range of teaching and learning activities they are likely to encounter, often with a focus on survival skills in the first few weeks, leading on to more reflective approaches later in the programme. However, few of these offer differing starting points throughout the year, to cope with academics who are appointed part-way through, and some exclude part-time, short-contract and temporary staff because of resource constraints. I was lucky to have Marcia to turn to as my informal mentor. Some universities have established first-rate formal mentoring schemes to supplement programmes or substitute for them when they are unavailable, and this is another strategy that is worth exploring.

What is clear is that both students and staff have a right to expect that new staff should get the help they need at the outset of their careers. New staff should not have to patch together a set of techniques for curriculum delivery by trial and error in the way I did. This will not eliminate disruptive behaviour but it will result in new staff feeling less exposed and vulnerable than I did, and will ensure that the quality of the students' learning experience is not impaired by lecturers learning their craft unaided.

CHAPTER 3

THE SMART STUDENT

Case reporter: Marilyn Baird

ISSUES RAISED

The issue raised in this case is that of lecturers having up-to-date knowledge and experience.

BACKGROUND

This case is set in the third year of a radiography course in a university of technology. The 36-year-old recently appointed female lecturer, previously a senior clinician, did not know that she would be expected to teach advanced radiographic procedures in which she had no clinical experience.

PART 1

Why did I leave what for me was an ideal working situation in the clinical setting? I was in my third year as chief radiographer of a busy radiology department situated in a prestigious private hospital. I enjoyed working with highly professional medical practitioners and nursing staff who valued my clinical knowledge and abilities. We had also recently become accredited as a clinical training centre for the local technical college and I had successfully supervised a second-year radiography student in the first half of the year.

Unfortunately in late spring of that fateful year, the radiology contact was renegotiated and to my dismay the consulting radiologists were replaced. I was offered a senior position in one of their small branches in the suburbs but I prevaricated as I enjoyed hospital work. I decided to adopt a wait and see policy. The new radiologists were pleasant but I missed the old team. I still did not know what I should do.

As spring gave way to summer I came across the agenda for the final Technical College Clinical Studies' meeting of the year. Because we had not had a student that semester I decided to phone to register an apology. To my surprise, Jack, the lecturer in charge of the clinical studies' programme, suggested I apply for the lecturer position in radiography that had recently been advertised. Why not I thought? After all, as Jack intimated, here was an opportunity to stay in my clinical area of expertise and embark upon a teaching career. Looking back, I remember feeling quite elated at the prospect of changing direction. The interviews were held early in December.

The week before Christmas Jack rang me. I had not actually got the position that was advertised but he wanted me to consider accepting a contract lecturing position that would still allow me to participate in the delivery of the general radiography component of the syllabus and the clinical studies subject. I decided to accept the position.

I knew I would have a lot to learn. Firstly, I did not have a clear under-standing of the curriculum of the three-year diploma course. I was an overseas trained radiographer. My only contact with the Tech had been through the Clinical Studies' Committee meetings. Secondly, I qualified as a radiographer back in 1971 before the digital revolution in medical imaging and my immediate clinical experience comprised mainly general film-based radiography. As the years had gone by, any clinical skills I had developed in the rapidly expanding area of computed tomography (CT) had slipped away. Yet I kept thinking does this lack of clinical experience really matter? After all I was going to teach students basic techniques and assist in their clinical education, was I not?

I took up the position at end of January. Despite my age I still felt nervous as I made my way to the staff room to meet Paul, the head of the department, and Charles, one of the senior lecturers. Over a coffee, Paul and Charles discussed the new degree course that was going to be introduced the following year. I remember Paul saying, 'You know Marilyn you are really joining us at the right time.' However, nothing was said about the content of what I would be teaching and how I might go about preparing for my role. Apparently, they wanted to wait until Jack arrived. After coffee, I was shown to a small empty office without a window. There was not a soul in sight down the long corridor. I remember sitting at the desk wondering what next? After the bustle of hospital life the office was deathly quiet.

Eventually Jack called me into his office. By the time I got there Charles had appeared and finally they told me what I was expected to do. 'Marilyn we were so impressed with the enthusiasm you demonstrated for angiography during the interview, that we have decided to give you the opportunity to teach the entire angiographic syllabus,' Jack said. Before I could catch my breath, Charles went on to say, 'We also think you should be able to teach CT as it's about time we expanded that part of our syllabus in preparation for next year.' To my dismay my teaching role in general radiography was to be confined to running laboratory-based practical sessions and assuming responsibility for the clinical visiting duties associated with third-year clinical studies. I was taken aback. I was in a difficult position. I had given up a senior clinical position and another similar position would be difficult to find. Hence, I was reluctant to admit just how little I knew. When I asked Jack, 'How would I teach CT given my lack of experience?' the reply was 'Well you only have to deliver a few lectures and you can always get a practitioner in to do it. You'll be fine.' The implicit assumption was that students would pick up all they really needed to know during their clinical rotation.

As I walked back down the corridor, I knew deep down that my clinical experience was not up to the task of teaching students the principles and practice of advanced imaging methods. I was aware of the fact that it is one thing to produce images of the blood vessels of the head and neck and legs and another thing to stand up and deliver a series of lectures on the entire topic. I would have been competent to lecture on general radiography, but I knew I would be unable to give my lectures in advanced imaging methods the clinical flavour students had the right to expect.

I still do not know why I stayed beyond that first week. I became increasingly worried about the prospect of working out what I should actually teach and the quality of my own knowledge base in respect to these aspects of advanced radiographic practice. Fortunately later that week I found sets of written material that had been developed by my predecessor and had been used in the delivery of the course to external students.

I decided to deal with angiography first and work out a lecture schedule. I went to the library and got out as many texts as I could find. I remember that during that first week all I did was read and read, including the lecture notes I had been given as a student. As I looked over the typewritten notes, I reflected upon my own learning experience. I simply recall it as a period of unmitigated boredom sitting in a flat-floor classroom listening to lecturer after lecturer droning on about aspects of practice that left us wondering if they had ever witnessed them. How the wheel turns! Now I was in a similar position. Was I going to inflict a similar experience upon students?

The more I read about angiography the more I became overwhelmed by the content. There was so much material to cover. Although I had some clinical experience, I could now see how much richer that experience could have been had I been exposed to the material I was now covering. I became determined, for instance, that my students would understand the dynamics of blood flow so they could select the correct timing sequence for capturing the flow of contrast media on film. Therefore, the key puzzle for me to solve was how to present this enormous amount of content to students in a lecture format without boring them.

I was keen to attend the two-day general induction course for new lecturers held in mid-February. I wanted to learn about teaching techniques. However, the course was too general and seemed to focus more upon the correct colour to use when writing overheads. Instead of being provided with strategies to improve student learning, the course supported the tacit assumption that the role of a university lecturer was to impart knowledge and examine the extent to which students retained this knowledge.

Fortunately, I was half way through a Bachelor of Arts degree that I was completing as an external student. The quality of the material sent out to students was extremely high and provided me with ideas on engaging students in the content material. For example, at the end of each topic we were given self-directed exercises to complete together with model answers. In addition, we were provided with selected readings to assist in connecting the facts with the wider political, economic and historical context. Time constraints did not allow me to adapt this approach to my initial lectures. I did, however, begin to assemble a set of learning folders containing a variety of scholarly research articles and methods articles which students might find useful. Moreover, because the date of my first lecture was fast approaching I decided to structure the delivery of the content around the headings developed by my predecessor.

When I think back, at no time did any of my colleagues suggest that I might benefit from an examination of their lecture notes and materials. The notion of peer supervision was foreign to them. This period and indeed my entire first year could best be described as a 'rite de passage'. The wider institution assumed that content expertise was synonymous with lecturing expertise. Moreover, the non-clinical staff with whom I worked made the automatic assumption that since I was clinically competent in general radiography I was competent in other aspects of practice as well.

I still vividly remember that first lecture in which Jack introduced me to the class. I looked up to see 40 faces peering down at me. It was just like being on stage. I was extraordinarily nervous and I know I spoke far too quickly. What was worse, the students were given no indication from me as to what they were to do. Were they expected to listen to me or write down everything I said? All I know is that I simply focused upon delivering the material in as short a time as possible. I avoided any eye contact with the students and I was very grateful for the fact that the tiered nature of the lecture room created a real distance between them and me.

The entire first semester was devoted to angiography and while I covered the content reasonably well, at the back of my mind there was always the fear that a student would ask me a clinically oriented question that I would be unable to answer. There were times when I struggled as much as the students did in making sense of the lecture material. I used videos from equipment suppliers and guest lecturers to cover the gaps in my clinical knowledge. This was not the perfect solution because student feedback indicated that the practitioner assumed students had more clinical experience in CT than they actually had. As a result, some students found it difficult to make sense of the material.

The following year saw the beginning of the new degree course. Spurred on by the example of my own undergraduate studies I knew that changes to my lectures would be needed. A different sort of practitioner was expected to emerge from the new degree-level education. At the same time, there had been a rapid increase in the clinical use of CT and improvements in the technology necessitating an update in my lecture material and an increase in the time devoted to it. In general radiography I felt equipped to meet the challenges posed by the new degree students, especially since I was now working a late shift in the casualty radiology room at a large public hospital.

I first met Adrian in the second-year radiography laboratory classes. It soon became obvious to me that I was dealing with a student who could best be described as a smart Alec. Everything I said or did in the class was challenged. If I told the students, a certain centring point was required for a particular radiographic projection then Adrian would want to know why. There was nothing wrong with this. However, because of the sarcastic way in which he couched his questions, I could never be sure whether he was genuinely concerned in developing a deeper understanding of basic radiographic positioning methods or he just asked questions to try to trip me up.

I also saw Adrian during clinical visiting. The supervising radiographer was impressed with Adrian's technical knowledge but expressed concern about his interpersonal skills and rapport with patients. I noted these concerns. However, I felt the radiographer's expectations were out of line given Adrian's limited clinical experience. Whilst I did not particularly like the student, I was nevertheless his mentor and my role was to ensure that he received appropriate clinical experience. I attempted to get Adrian to try to see how radiographers might interpret his actions and general demeanour. I stressed the need for him to consider the patient as his first priority.

I remember the CT lecture well. It was the second lecture in a series on CT technology, positioning principles and imaging protocols. In this lecture I intended to outline the key features of the equipment students would need to familiarize themselves with during their clinical rotation. I was half way through the lecture, which was being listened to attentively by the students, when I mentioned the gantry into which the patient is placed. I told students that in CT examinations of the head they could angle the gantry to overcome positioning difficulties a patient might have. My diagram illustrated the point and I was about to move on when Adrian spoke out in a loud and dismissive voice: 'You haven't shown that correctly. Your diagram shows the gantry being angled towards the patient's feet. Don't you know it can be angled the other way as well? That would certainly be better with this patient.' I froze. I could not believe that after all my hard work in preparing myself that I had made what appeared to be a fundamental error in respect to the movement of the gantry.

What was I to do now? While I always encouraged students to participate in the lecture, I did not expect comments that could best be described as 'smart'. In one fell swoop Adrian's remark shot a hole in my credibility as an academic. I knew I could not just walk out of the lecture even though I felt like doing it. I certainly remember wishing the ground would open and swallow me up. I felt so alone with a sea of faces looking to see what I would do next. I was angry with myself for failing to appreciate the capabilities of the gantry during my visits to one of the clinical CT departments. Neither had any of the textbooks I used as support for my lectures stressed the fact that the gantry could be angled in either direction. I was also angry with Adrian for being so smart and showing me up. At the same time, I felt I had let the students down. How could they trust anything else I might say about CT following such an incident?

- How would you handle this situation?
- What do you think the teacher actually did next?

PART 2

In what seemed like an eternity, I coped with the situation by thanking Adrian and admitting that I had not previously appreciated the full extent of the gantry movements. I remember then addressing the other topics I intended to cover in the lecture. Finally, the lecture was over and I gathered up my overheads and left the lecture theatre. On the way back to my room, I carefully avoided any direct contact with the students. Again, I was grateful for the distance the tiered lecture theatre provided between the students and me.

I went back to my room and shut the door. I was upset. I became angry with senior members of the department and their lack of recognition of the need for the continuing and ongoing clinical development of their staff. The incident confirmed my earlier fears concerning my lack of clinical experience in CT. Yet, I had undertaken plenty of visits to clinical sites. I began to realize that observation without active participation does not necessarily lead to the construction of meaningful knowledge and understanding. No wonder the profession was concerned with the huge reduction in clinical hours in the new course. Theory can never teach you how to practice. I began to appreciate that it is only when you have to implement something in a practical sense that you begin to recognize the difference between knowing *that* and knowing *how*.

How was I to resolve the situation and regain credibility in the eyes of the students? I was now in my third year as a lecturer, so how could I now go out into the clinical world and admit that I still did not fully understand the workings of the machinery. Through my clinical visits, I was widely known within the profession and I had become involved with the professional body, convening continuing education seminars. One way of resolving the situation could have been through the creation of a CT laboratory on campus. However there was no money for such an innovation and, anyway, I seemed to be the only person in the department who worried about the need to have clinical abilities.

In the end, I decided to create a video on the principles and practice of CT using a unit in a large teaching hospital. Through making the video, I learned the nuances of CT imaging and could provide students with a clinical context at key points of the lecture. As I now realized, when you have no clinical experience using particular methods or machinery the words spoken by the lecturer have no meaning. Students also have nothing against which to reflect the points being made by the lecturer. The process of writing the script and directing the various scenes in the video restored my confidence as a lecturer and improved my own knowledge and understanding of third-generation CT scanning. I also resolved to make strategic use in the lecture programme of expert radiographers and technical support staff from the various X-ray companies who manufactured the equipment.

Then just as I was feeling more secure another technological revolution in CT occurred. However, this time I was lucky. The advent of helical or so-called spiral CT scanning coincided with the need for the department to employ another radiography lecturer. There was no mistake this time. The person selected for the position had up-to-date clinical skills in this area and was encouraged to maintain those skills through the mechanism of a joint clinical and university appointment. This was due in no small part to the fact that I was now the coordinator of the diagnostic radiography programme. I was finally in a position to effect change to the way in which the lectures would be delivered.

- How well do you think the teacher coped with the situation?
- If faced with a similar incident how would you have acted?
- Was the teacher's assessment of the situation too extreme?
- What is your general approach to challenges or questions from students that you are unable to answer immediately?

DISCUSSION

How could I have avoided this situation? For example, could I have read more widely? Well, many authors make unrealistic assumptions about the prior knowledge of their readers and in so doing tend to gloss over certain fundamental principles. At the same time, textbooks have the habit of describing only the ideal examination with the ideal patient. Perhaps instead of working a late shift in general radiography, I could have moved out of my comfort zone and applied to do a shift operating the CT scanner? Yet, there were personal risks involved in this strategy. Lecturers are human beings too.

To reveal to experienced clinicians the limits of my knowledge and understanding may have diminished my credibility in the eyes of my peers. Such an admission would raise legitimate questions about my knowledge and expertise.

The entire higher education enterprise is based upon the assumption that lecturers possess sound knowledge about something and their role is to assist students to become just as knowledgeable. Nevertheless, while this assumption may hold in traditional disciplines, it becomes untenable in the context of preparing students for entry into professions in which knowing how is as important as knowing that. In health care professions, clinical experience is fundamental to the construction of practical knowledge.

Universities have always had difficulty in dealing with the delivery of courses designed to prepare students for entry into a professional practice. The traditional medical curriculum, with its clear division between the preclinical and clinical components of the course, represents one approach to managing this challenge. However, this approach is based upon rationalist notions of professional action and the idea that practitioners directly apply scientific knowledge to the resolution of practical problems. Since the 1980s, research into student learning and the nature of clinical knowing has revealed serious flaws in this model (Schön, 1987; Fish and Twinn, 1997). It is now recognized that professional practice actually draws upon different forms of knowledge (Higgs and Tichen, 1995).

The attitude of the university to the construction of professional curricula conveniently ignores the fact that through experience and reflecting, thinking practitioners construct a personal form of knowledge about what they do. Moreover, in busy practice settings expert clinicians do not necessarily engage in a hypothetical, deductive form of reasoning; they simply enact what works for them. And this largely 'tacit' form of knowledge is 'embedded' in their actions. Practice cannot be separated out into distinct particles of knowledge. The nature of practical action and the unpredictability of the practice situation therefore make it impossible for propositional knowledge to be used 'off the shelf'.

Thus, the notion that theory delivered in a lecture room can be effortlessly integrated with practical know-how is flawed. What the 'technocratic' model of professional education fails to understand is that the classroom and the clinic are not synonymous (Balla, 1989). The assumption by traditional academics that lectures designed to provide students with information to be used in the clinical setting could legitimately be given by someone without clinical experience is misguided.

Clearly a more effective model of professional education is one in which students are taught by practitioner lecturers who are able to draw upon their clinical experiences in realistic and valid ways and assist students to make those vital connections between scientific theories and clinical practice. As I found out, a smart student will sooner or later catch out the unsuspecting lecturer. The case shows the risks that lecturers in professional courses take when their clinical experience is out of kilter with the topic they are teaching.

The incident described in this case happened early in my teaching career and made me feel very inadequate at the time. On more mature reflection, I now realize that ALL lecturers teaching ALL subjects will be challenged or asked a question they cannot answer immediately even if they are incredibly well prepared. What do you as a lecturer do when you inevitably get the question you cannot answer or a student shows you are wrong on something? Are you comfortable not to be the font of all knowledge? Rather than worrying about the threat of 'being wrong' are you able to model for students the wish to learn and improve yourself – the thirst for knowledge irrespective of who provides it?

This case highlights the need for universities to ensure that former practitioners who enter the academy are given the opportunity to maintain and, where necessary, enhance their clinical knowledge and skills. The lecture setting is a useful forum in assisting students to develop the framework against which they can reflect their clinical experiences. However, the success or otherwise of the lecture in achieving meaningful learning outcomes for students is related to the clinical experience of the lecturer.

REFERENCES

Balla, J I (1989) Changing concepts in clinical education: the case for a theory, in *Learning in Medical School*, ed J I Balla, M Gibson and A M Chang, Hong Kong University Press, Hong Kong

Fish, D and Twinn, S (1997) *Quality Clinical Supervision in the Health Care Professions*, Butterworth Heinemann, Oxford

Higgs, J and Titchen, A (1995) Propositional, professional and personal knowledge in clinical reasoning, in *Clinical Reasoning in the Health Professions*, ed J Higgs and M Jones, Butterworth Heinemann, Oxford

Schön, D A (1987) *Educating the Reflective Practitioner*, Jossey-Bass, San Francisco

CHAPTER 4

THE MOBILE PHONE

Case reporters: Brian Hinton and Catherine Manathunga[1]

ISSUES RAISED

This case study explores the challenge of dealing with a disruptive student in the lecture context and examines the extent of lecturers' rights in the face of confronting student behaviour. It focuses on the 'modern' dilemma of dealing with mobile phones during lectures.

BACKGROUND

The incident on which this case study is based occurred at an Australian university in the 1990s. The male lecturer was in his 40s, teaching a second-year undergraduate subject in information technology. Prior to teaching in universities, the lecturer had 10 years experience with IBM, travelling the world as a support software engineer working with multinational corporations. The information technology subject he was teaching when the incident took place was perceived by students as particularly difficult and was known for its high failure rate. The majority of students were aged between 18 and 21.

PART 1

The day started much like any other in my teaching life. My mood was ambivalent and a cigarette and two coffees did not swing things either way. It was raining outside and I had three lectures to get through. Little did I realize that today had been chosen, by whoever decides these things, to be a minor seminal event in my life.

I started into my first lecture, explaining some quite complex and very dry information technology material. It was in the area of data communications protocols, which, for the un-IT-initiated, involves the internal programming of computer network technologies. The lecture theatre was a dark, drab, tiered room, seating about 200 students, with a fixed podium at the front and no fancy technology at all.

The students found the material difficult and were concentrating hard. It was about ten minutes into the lecture that I first noticed a student tapping away on a mobile phone. He was a very tall and large young man named Gary. He was wearing the typical student attire of the time: a T-shirt featuring a heavy metal rock band and jeans. It was apparent that he was beginning to annoy nearby students. Apart from the tapping, the mobile phone was making continual low-level beeping noises. Students kept turning around, staring at him and rolling their eyes at the distracting noise he was making.

I was quite intrigued as to why anyone would tap away, seemingly endlessly, on a mobile phone. I stopped the lecture. I do not normally take this action but I was becoming mildly irritated by the noise. I asked politely, 'What are you doing, Gary?', to which Gary replied, totally nonplussed, 'I'm playing a game on my mobile phone.'

Firmly, I said, 'Gary, please stop playing with your mobile phone.' With a condescending sneer on his face and confrontational posture, Gary replied, 'Yeah, OK.' I could see he was spoiling for a fight but hoped that he had gotten his attention fix and would settle down.

Five minutes later, however, Gary was tapping away at the mobile phone again. My internal irritation barometer was rising but I did not want to give Gary the satisfaction of knowing this. Once more, I took the unusual action of stopping the lecture. Remaining polite, I said, 'Gary, stop playing with your mobile phone. You are distracting me and annoying your classmates.' I wanted him to know he was now overstepping the boundaries of acceptable classroom behaviour. His attention-seeking behaviour was inhibiting other students' learning. Gary insolently replied once again, 'Yeah, OK.' The students sensed that a confrontation was brewing. The atmosphere seemed close and tense. Some students seemed keen to see the drama played out; a welcome relief from the intense concentration required mastering this aspect of computer programming.

Lo and behold, a few minutes later Gary decided to make a telephone call and began chatting away to a 'mate'. By now my irritation level was rising rapidly, but I remembered my industry training and kept my anger hidden behind a calm surface veneer. Once again, I stopped the lecture. I waited for the conversation to end, as Gary had no intention of interrupting his phone call for me. It was only a few minutes but it seemed like a day.

'Right, Gary,' I said, 'since lectures are not compulsory and we are in an adult learning environment, believe it or not, I suggest that you leave this class. Go down to the student union or somewhere else. You can play your games or make phone calls in peace and let us get on with this class!'

Gary then stood up. A deathly hush descended on the class. The atmosphere of excitement changed to nervous expectation. Students sat bolt upright
in their chairs, wide-eyed and frozen to the spot. I should point out that Gary
was well over six feet tall and weighed around two hundred and fifty pounds.
I, on the other hand, just reach six feet on a good day and have a slim build.

Gary, sneering aggressively, proceeded to utter 'Yeah' and sat back down
again. The inevitable happened after another three or four minutes. He
started up on his mobile phone game again! This had gone from the sublime
to way past the ridiculous. It was now a straight out, no holds barred, contest
for supremacy!

What do I do now?

- What do you think the teacher did next?
- What would you have done at this point?

PART 2

I knew I had to take immediate action to retain authority. While the drama
was unfolding, I thought about my next course of action. I had wanted to
give Gary the benefit of the doubt but I sensed from the beginning that a
confrontation was likely. So I announced to the class that I wanted them to
take a break and then remain outside until I called them back into the room.
I do not know what they expected me to do, but I did not want to divide my
attention between thinking about how to deal with Gary and playing to any
audience. They filed out quickly. While some seemed relieved, others were
slightly disappointed at missing the action. At no time did I get a sense that
they supported Gary's actions.

'Gary,' I declared resolutely, 'Stay here, thank you.' I had never taken this
type of action before but I could now think of no other way of resolving the
situation. In reality, it was a frightening conflict that had to be resolved
without there being a clear winner if pride was to be maintained on both
sides. I needed to regain control of the classroom but there was no point in
making an enemy of the students.

I told Gary, 'There is no way I will allow you to remain here for the rest of
the lecture. I will call security to escort you from the room if you do not
remove yourself.' I further pointed out, calmly, 'If I have to call security, I
will need to report this to the head of school. Further draconian sanctions can
be taken if we want to, Gary.' Although it was a scary situation, I spoke slowly
and calmly, keeping my body language relaxed but attentive. I deliberately
kept my hands down by my sides, ensuring that I did not clench my fists or
give out any other threatening signals.

I remembered the GOLDEN RULE – always leave pride intact if possible.
I did not give the student a chance to reply as I could see he was getting

angry. Very calmly I said, 'We all have situations that upset us. Sometimes we have things on our minds that stop us concentrating. I'm sure you must be dealing with some difficult issues right now.' I could see the look on his face soften. The muscles in his face relaxed as he recognized that I had offered him a way out of this situation. He was smart enough to know that, this time, he had gone way too far. As a sweetener, I said, 'Gary, I can't let you stay for the rest of the lecture, but I am happy to see you in a few days time to give you some work to catch up on lost time.'

Nodding quietly, he left the class and, happily enough, I never experienced any more difficulties with Gary in later classes.

Breathing a sigh of relief, I called the other students back into the lecture theatre. Abbreviating the material a bit, I finished the lecture. The students were unusually quiet and attentive. I did not seek any feedback from the students about the incident. I believe that these situations are best forgotten quickly. They should not be exaggerated or glorified. I did notice, however, that, for a few weeks at least, all the students remained more attentive and respectful in class. Unfortunately, this did not last forever!

- How well do you think the teacher handled this incident?
- If faced with a similar incident, how would you have acted?
- What would you have done differently?

DISCUSSION

This case study raises some of the dilemmas faced by lecturers in the new century as they teach large classes with high numbers of 'Generation X' students. For these students, the mobile phone has become, in many cases, a necessity of life and even a central feature of their identity. To be un-contactable, even for a brief period, can be akin to social paralysis or death. Using mobile phones is as normal as breathing. In this way, many students do not consider the impact that their use of mobile phones in lectures has on other students and on the lecturer.

The student in this case study, however, was not content just to make a social call during the lecture. This in itself is highly disruptive and should not be tolerated. He also insisted on playing games on his mobile phone, which was even worse because of the constant tapping and beeping. Again, this is partly a generational issue. 'Generation X' students are used to constant and rapidly changing stimulation, as Wagschal (1997) and Johnson and Orr (1999) indicate. If a lecture does not grab their attention in 8 seconds and hold that attention throughout the remaining hour or two, many younger students feel constrained by inactivity. Not content merely to daydream, they want constant, interactive, often visual stimulation and this need can boil over into disruptive behaviour if it is not satisfied. A recent study on the use of multimedia in large lectures indicated the vital role played by 'the inclusion of sound, movement, [and] pictures' in lectures in captivating and motivating the 'MTV generation' (Pippert and Moore, 1999: 7). The dynamics of this equation will no doubt change once more 'Generation X' lecturers start teaching.

While these new generational factors are central to this case study, the issues underlying it are as old as teaching itself. They focus on acceptable classroom behaviour and teacher control. In the past, lecturers expected that students inherently understood the boundaries of acceptable classroom behaviour. In Brian's experience, even five years ago, many students were more conscious of these boundaries. Previously, lecturers assumed that students would quietly take notes while they delivered a monologue. This fitted with the notion that teaching was about information delivery, retention and regurgitation. If students opted to push those boundaries, which they have done since time immemorial, lecturers relied on their respected status to deal with unacceptable behaviour.

This hierarchical notion of teaching has thankfully been replaced. So too, our understanding of what learning is about and, therefore, how teaching can be constructed has changed. We have moved to a focus on encouraging deep approaches to learning, where students critically engage with their material (Marton, Dall'Alba and Beaty, 1993). This can be achieved by ensuring that students complete constructive learning activities that are carefully aligned with the curriculum objectives (Ramsden, 1992; Biggs, 1999). So, lecturers now work towards facilitating the students' understanding and engagement with material. We have access to technology that, if used thoughtfully, allows us to elaborate on our content in dramatic and powerful ways. We focus on breaking up our lectures with segments of interaction with and between our students.

All of these improvements, however, have changed the rules and process of the lecturing game. Because we are now able to demonstrate our humanity as we actively facilitate the students' learning, instead of merely imparting 'knowledge', we have to work harder to earn the respect of our students. The composition of our student audience has also changed so that we now teach large numbers of highly diverse students with a range of learning needs. We can no longer assume that students will automatically know what is acceptable or immediately accept our authority if they cross those boundaries of appropriate behaviour.

Brian was able to deal effectively with a difficult and potentially physically threatening student by being firm but fair. Although it was a frightening situation, Brian was able to call on his industry experience in dealing with difficult clients. He was able, once the other students had left the room, calmly to ask Gary to leave, while allowing him to salvage a modicum of pride by acknowledging that he must have had some serious issues on his mind. In this way, he was able to appear sympathetic and approachable. Brian also ensured that Gary would not be unduly penalized by being forced to leave the lecture theatre. By using this combination of firmness and understanding, he was able to earn Gary's respect so that he was cooperative for the rest of semester. He was also able to earn the respect of the other students whose learning was being disrupted during this incident. In this way, he was able to maintain his authority without alienating the disruptive student or the other members of the class.

To do so required a complicated balancing act. It was important that Brian retained control of the classroom. Had he ignored Gary's antics, he would have encouraged disruptive behaviour and, in the process, lost the respect of the whole class. Had he exploded or acted aggressively, the conflict could have escalated and he would certainly have alienated Gary. The other students may also have sided with Gary or, at the very least, found the spectacle amusing or disturbing.

This was a key learning experience for Brian. He recognized that he could no longer assume that students knew the boundaries of acceptable classroom behaviour, particularly in relation to the generational issue of mobile phones. He now takes some time to set the ground rules in the first lectures for each class. He specifies quite clearly that mobile phones are to be turned off during lecture times. If a student forgets to switch his or her phone off or is expecting a vital call in a genuine crisis situation, he asks that he or she leaves the lecture theatre before answering the call. Setting the ground rules clearly can also be used to try and deal with other more traditional inappropriate behaviours, such as eating in class, passing notes, talking and even reading the student newspaper – behaviour described by Carbone (1998).

In setting ground rules, Brian is careful to explain why each rule is necessary. An additional strategy, which may ensure that students respect these boundaries to a greater extent, is to involve them in the process of setting the ground rules for the class. The lecturer can still have several key non-negotiable rules like allowing only one person to speak at a time, not using put-downs, and not making sexist or racist jokes. But seeking the participation of students in setting ground rules acknowledges students as adult learners and gives them some degree of ownership of the classroom. Although setting the ground rules does not prevent all inappropriate behaviour in classes, it can stop some students from testing the boundaries.

Ground rules can also be turned into a learning contract or written agreement, which is then easy to refer to if students start to push the boundaries of acceptable behaviour. When this happens, documentation is required that can also be used to develop a departmental policy or statement. As with much else in teaching and learning, expectations that are clear, explicit and shared by staff and students tend to make it less likely that problems will arise.

QUESTIONS FOR PERSONAL REFLECTION

- Have you ever experienced a similar situation where you have had to deal with a disruptive student? What did you do?
- Have you experienced any particular challenges in teaching 'Generation X' students? Have you developed any strategies to keep 'Generation X' students occupied during lectures?
- Do you and your students set the ground rules for appropriate behaviour in your classes at the beginning of the semester?
- Are there any other implications or lessons to be drawn from this case that have application in your own teaching? Is there anything in your own teaching practice that you need to reconsider having read and reflected on this case?

NOTES

[1]This case study is based on Brian's experience, which was jointly analysed by Catherine and Brian.

REFERENCES

Biggs, J (1999) *Teaching for Quality Learning at University: What the student does*, Society for Research into Higher Education & Open University Press, Buckingham

Carbone, E (1998) *Teaching Large Classes: Tools and strategies*, Sage Publications, Thousand Oaks

Johnson, C and Orr, C (1999) Promoting the work ethic among Generation-X and N-Gen students, *National Business Education Yearbook*, **37**, pp 16–26

Marton, F, Dall'Alba, G and Beaty, E (1993) Conceptions of learning, *International Journal of Educational Research*, **19** (3), pp 277–300

Pippert, T and Moore, H (1999) Multiple perspectives on multimedia in the large lecture, *Teaching Sociology*, **27** (2), pp 92–109

Ramsden, P (1992) *Learning to Teach in Higher Education*, Routledge, London

Wagschal, K (1997) I became clueless teaching the GenXers, *Adult Learning*, **8** (4) pp 21–25

PART 2

ORCHESTRATING LEARNING IN LECTURES

CHAPTER 5

I FELL ASLEEP IN MY OWN LECTURE

Case reporter: Bob Lord

ISSUES RAISED

The key issue raised in this case study is challenging students to become researcher/discoverers rather than memorizers, within the mandatory academic structure of lecture/tutorial/laboratory.

BACKGROUND

This case is set in a compulsory, core, second-level course in telecommunications engineering at a large Australian university of technology. The students are mainly in their early 20s and have a diverse range of intellectual ability and interests. There are 300 students in the group and they come together for a one-hour lecture each week, a one-hour tutorial (48 students) every two weeks, and a two-hour laboratory session (24 students) every two weeks.

PART 1

I went to sleep in my own lecture! How embarrassing to be discovered by your partner fast asleep in front of the TV during a broadcast of your very own lecture! Let me tell you this is something that takes a very long time to live down. Being the butt of family jokes relating to this incident hurt my professional pride, so I decided that I would make my lectures more interesting and engaging to the audience. I wanted them to be as captivating as Julius Sumner Miller's TV series 'Why is it so?' that had engrossed me, and many of my contemporary colleagues, in our youth. But I am getting ahead of myself.

Increasing enrolments in my subject led to a request from the head of department to present each lecture twice as there was no theatre available large enough to accommodate the full class. The idea of repeating each lecture appealed to the head of department as it eased the timetabling problem that was created by the students from 12 different degrees taking my course. I persuaded him to allow me to provide a studio-produced video-taped lecture to support a single live lecture as a better solution to the conflicting timetable and accommodation problems. I argued that video-taped lectures were a step in the online flexible delivery direction. My hope was that enough students would choose the videotaped lecture option, allowing all desiring a live lecture to be accommodated at a single lecture session in the available theatre. The head of department reluctantly agreed and I was greatly relieved when subsequently about half the students chose the video option. The video innovation developed to the extent that Community Television MCT Channel 31 broadcast the videotaped lectures to the greater Melbourne area.

It was while monitoring one of the telecasts at home that I was caught napping. And this proved to be a critical incident in my academic career as a lecturer. The single most significant result for me from producing the video-taped version of my lecture series was that I saw my own lectures. I had to accept that while I had thought I was pretty good, in reality there was room for vast improvement.

So I took the videotapes of my 13-lecture series on Telecommunication Engineering to Dick Bilby, a respected TV science presenter/producer, to have them assessed. Dick was very critical of my productions and I felt my self-esteem seep away as Dick discussed my videos with me as if he was a film critic reporting on a second-rate movie. I was like a baby seal in a shark pool as he methodically went through each of my lectures, clearly and professionally, indicating four or five places in each lecture where the 'audience' would be lost. Each time I protested that these were important parts of the lesson, Dick would say, 'Bob it's your task to find an angle through which you can take your message to the audience without losing them. Most importantly you must convey the wonder of engineering to the audience.'

As I licked my wounds on the plane home, I reflected on that embarrassing afternoon with Dick Bilby. My very psyche had been stripped bare under the astute Bilby microscope. But Lecture 4 had impressed him. He also mentioned that his wife and children had paused to watch the 'Magic Lantern' demonstration in this lecture as he was reviewing the videotapes at home. I had developed the 'Magic Lantern' lecture demonstration over a number of years and knew that it created tremendous interest. It had become known as my 'gun' lecture by the technical and other staff in the department. This had always made me feel good and presenting this lecture, with the demonstration, had been a lot of fun over the years, as many people with a little knowledge of electricity are unable to explain what is happening.

I was seriously challenged by Dick Bilby and wanted to use more demonstrations in my lectures to replace the detailed verbal explanations and mathematical derivations that had put me to sleep. Dick had repeatedly identified these sections as being the 'problem' areas of the lecture presentation. In fact, it was during one of these very mathematical derivations that I had nodded off, so I knew Dick was pointing me in the right direction.

I had many ideas for lecture demonstrations and began to develop some custom-made equipment set-ups for this purpose, but I did not use them in lectures as I lacked the courage. I was afraid that the equipment would fail, something would go wrong or that the students would not see the point of what I was showing them. However, I desperately wanted to make a more active attempt to engage the class, and wider TV audience, through the greater use of action and activity by me, initially, using activities such as live demonstrations and interactive computer simulations.

But would such an approach degrade the course into a series of 'Mickey Mouse' entertainment sessions? The sessions may hold the audience's interest, and be great fun, but would the content be forgotten as quickly as that of a TV soap opera, or a traditional engineering lecture? If lectures are to be made more interesting, engaging, interactive and entertaining, can they be considered in isolation from the remainder of the educational programme, the tutorials and laboratory classes, in the course.

The apparent conflict between making lectures interesting and telling students what they have to know, was rattling around in my head when I read the following:

> Nearly every subject has a shadow, or imitation. It would, I suppose, be quite possible to teach a deaf and dumb child to play the piano. When it played a wrong note, it would see the frown of its teacher, and try again. But it would obviously have no idea of what it was doing, or why anyone should devote hours to such an extraordinary exercise. It would have learnt an imitation of music. And it would have learnt to fear the piano exactly as most students fear what is supposed to be mathematics.
> (Sawyer, in Ramsden, 1992, Chapter 4)

I was struck by this concept of imitations and shadows when applied to teaching and wondered whether I was an imitation teacher, rounding up students like a dog rounding up sheep, when I should be more like a Pied Piper enticing students to follow me. I feared I was the former and decided I wanted to change into the latter. However, if I did not tell students what they had to know, how would they ever find out? Worse still, how would I know that they had found out? How was I going to make the lecture more interesting and yet maintain the academic credibility of the course? How would the students learn the mathematical models upon which engineering relies?

- The use of demonstrations in a lecture makes the lecture more interesting but reduces the time available to present the course subject matter. How can these conflicting requirements be reconciled?
- What do you think the lecturer will do to develop interesting demonstrations in the lecture and yet satisfy the demand for detailed technical and mathematical information?
- How do you think the lecturer can actually make his lectures more interesting?

PART 2

I wrestled for more than a year with the apparent conflict between making my lectures more interesting and using the time to tell students what they needed to know. My thoughts kept returning to Sawyer's quote. I did not want to train imitation engineers; I wanted to educate real professional engineers.

Then it happened!

I attended a weekend workshop with Edward de Bono and a team of Australian engineering educationalists. There, I enthusiastically embraced a model for personal action developed by Jim Butler (Edwards *et al*, 1997). Butler's model distinguishes between the 'external to self' public taught knowledge that is seen in public performance and the 'internal to self' private belief and value system and personal practical knowledge that is internal to the person. This model is consistent with Sawyer's imitations and shadows in that it draws a distinction between the personal knowledge and world view that we each have, and public (or taught) knowledge and performance.

It became clear to me, as I reflected on Butler's model, that 'external to self' activities were what happened in the lectures and that I wanted to access 'internal to self' activities. I concluded that personal practical knowledge gained from real life experiences and set within the framework of the individual's belief and value system was overwhelmingly more powerful in an individual's learning than anything he or she was told. I was sold on the idea as I think it matched my 'gut feeling' or, as Jim Butler would say, my own personal practical knowledge.

To try to gain access to Butler's 'internal to self' side of learning I decided to make the student activities in the laboratory the new focus for the learning programme rather than my activities in the lecture. Lecture demonstrations can provide a strong link between the scientific theories espoused in the lecture time slot (public knowledge) and the laboratory exercises performed by the students (personal practical knowledge) in the laboratory time slot. The Butler model gave me the clue that demonstration-based lectures could be combined with investigative laboratory project work to promote deep approaches to learning (in the Ramsden, 1992 sense).

Everything began to fit into place for me now. I became really excited and decided to aim my learning programme at building a learner's personal knowledge and changing his or her world view. Such a programme simply demanded that lectures be biased away from a didactic theory of knowledge (ie teach WHAT to think rather than HOW to think) and be biased towards a reflective theory of knowledge (ie teach HOW to think rather than WHAT to think) (Lord, 1998). The role of the lecture became to excite and engage the students rather than to 'teach' them.

The Julius Sumner Miller inspired lectures were enthusiastically received. 'Bob, they love you!' said the e-mail from associate professor Carmel McNaught as she reported the results of the first focus group interview with volunteers from the student group. Lectures were now much more fun for me and for the audience, even though they now aimed at the much more challenging task of influencing the learner's internal world view. Regular student feedback revealed the lecture demonstrations as the key aspect of the lecture that most assisted student learning in the subject. Associate professor David Jamieson from the School of Physics at the University of Melbourne and a winner of an outstanding teacher award notes that his 'students consistently report this is one of the best things about physics – that we have well-organized, live demonstrations' (Ridgway and Richiardi, 1998). Reports such as these built my confidence and deepened my commitment to my new approach to lecturing.

The response from my students fed my enthusiasm and the demonstrations soon became the focus for the entire lecture, in fact the entire learning programme for each topic under discussion. I set about the demanding task of preparing a demonstration for each lecture.

A key to my developing teaching style was what I call 'learning engines'. A 'learning engine' is a basic real (and/or virtual) interactive experimental set-up that is used by me in lecture demonstrations, by students in groups during tutorial and/or laboratory times, or individually by students in their own time. The use of each new learning engine requires the learner to invest some time and effort to understand the engine itself. The engine is then used progressively, in the lecture as a demonstration, in the tutorial as a simulation, and in the laboratory for real-world measurements. This series of different uses of the same 'learning engine' provides a familiar learning environment to which additional complexities can be added progressively. In this way, learners extend their understanding to embrace each new complexity as it is introduced in the lecture time and developed further during the tutorial and laboratory times.

I developed 'virtual learning engines', software simulations of the lecture demonstrations, so that students could work at home, or in tutorials, to build their personal knowledge before coming to the laboratory session. This raised the profile of laboratory work considerably and students came to the laboratory session with a better understanding of what was to be done.

Laboratory time was spent more productively than when the students were following traditional recipe type engineering laboratory experiments.

I now spend most of my time developing learning engines, rather than preparing detailed mathematical derivations and explanations of complicated scientific theories for presentation in the lecture. I found developing learning engines to be much more fun as it involves teasing out the crucial underlying concepts and principles of each lecture topic and coming up with a practical demonstration to highlight the concept. I love puzzles and try to design learning engines that give counter-intuitive results. Technical staff join in the fun of trying to create situations that produce results that are contradictory to those predicted by a naive understanding of the phenomenon being examined. Visitors to the department are curious about what we are doing and many become 'guinea pigs' for our provocative questions and contribute their thoughts. It seems that such questioning activity is irresistible to academics and technical staff alike. But are such activities also irresistible to undergraduate students?

To engage the lecture class more with the demonstrations I began using a 'predict, observe, and explain' learning methodology. I asked the students in the lecture what would happen when I did something with the learning engine. I usually asked them to discuss this with their neighbour for one minute and to make a commitment to what they thought would happen. During this time, I had a chance to check or adjust the equipment. I then performed the action and everyone observed the result. If students had predicted the outcome correctly, then the mathematical model they used in their prediction was all right and they were ready to move forward. If their prediction was incorrect, their mathematical model needed 'adjustment'.

I also tried to end each lecture with a demonstration of some new puzzling phenomenon that I left with the class without explanation but telling them 'that all will be revealed in the next session'.

The predict, observe and explain methodology was also encouraged in the investigative laboratory projects to help students integrate the scientific theories outlined in lectures with the personal knowledge and world view being developed in the laboratories and tutorials. During tutorials the 'virtual learning engines' were used to check predictions of the mathematical models against observations of the simulation outcome.

Everything went really well during the semester and I was feeling very pleased with myself when I sat down to prepare the final examination question paper. This was a new challenge as the old memory recall 'tell me what I told you' paper was not appropriate. Would my assessment have to change? I have always wanted to assess whether or not the learner had mastered a new conceptual understanding by testing what the learner can do with the new concept, in particular whether the student could use the concept to predict the outcome of an unfamiliar situation. When I looked back at my previous examination question papers they tended to be the 'tell me what I told you in lectures' type. With the lecture time taken up by demonstrations and interactive computer simulation activity there had been much less time to tell the class this type of information. Students might complain that I was asking questions on the examination paper that had not been covered in lectures.

The examination had to test whether the students could perform the mathematical calculations and derivations as they had in the past and I did not want all my students to fail, as this would be an indication to my peers that what I was doing was unsatisfactory.

What was I to do?

- How would you attempt to examine students who had been taught in this way?
- What do you think actually happened to students in the examination?

PART 3

I modified the assessment in two major ways to reward students who practised a reflective theory of knowledge by seeking understanding ahead of memorizing. Firstly, students were encouraged to study a smaller number of topics but to a greater depth by selecting three projects from the six available in each semester for detailed investigation in the laboratory time slot. Two or three lecture sessions provided the background discussion for each of the six projects. Secondly, the formal written examination was completely open book, and students were free to take any written textual material into the examination with them. There was one question on each of the six project areas and students could attempt any three questions.

The fact that any one student might not understand the entire subject syllabus content, as presented in the lectures, did not concern me as the focus was on the fundamentals. The same fundamentals underlie each of the six topics (otherwise they are not fundamentals are they?) and a student could demonstrate understanding of the fundamentals through an in-depth understanding of any topic. Incidentally, lecture attendance remained solidly above 90 per cent of the class even though students were well aware of the choice available to them.

I was amazed and greatly relieved by the results of the independently moderated final examination. The majority of students had learned the mathematics without detailed presentations of this material in lectures. There were 99 high distinctions (above 80 per cent), with 10 students scoring 100 per cent. But, at the other end of the scale, 66 students, from a total of 271 candidates, failed, scoring less than the pass mark of 50 per cent. This rather flat distribution contrasted with the 'bell-shaped curve' results of previous years.

A significant minority of students had been unable to cope with the learning style of the revised learning programme. These students had made very little progress and stratified focus group interviews confirmed that the poorly performing students were not coping with the revised programme.

It seemed that the lecture programme, laboratory instructions, and assessment based on a reflective theory of knowledge overwhelmed some students and they became 'lost' and performed poorly. They wanted to be told what they had to learn and how they were supposed to learn it. This substantial minority of students (approximately 20 per cent) may have fared better under traditional university instruction but experienced difficulties learning from exercises designed for learners as researcher/discoverers. They were not well prepared and failed to adapt to the researcher/discover role required by the revised programme.

Dealing with this under-performing student group has now become my work in progress.

DISCUSSION

The majority of the students related positively to the new approach to their learning, as reported regularly in the annual Departmental Student Commissioned Quality Reports. Both the lectures and the laboratory programme are rated as 'excellent', with the feedback identifying that the 'predict, observe, explain' learning strategy worked really well in lecture demonstrations and laboratory projects. The focus group interviews reported that the lecture demonstrations 'were the key learning feature of the lectures', for both live and video lectures. It was also clear from student survey feedback that the laboratory projects were where the learners felt that most of their learning was taking place in the revised learning programme.

I now think that a successful lecture motivates the class to choose from the student activities provided, and to uncover the understanding necessary to take the mathematically based models that underpin the lecture, into their new understanding of the world. Exercising the flexible learning materials is the means by which the learners come to their new understanding of the topic. The learner remodels and refines their world view through the gaining of personal practical knowledge and reflecting on these activities within the framework of the public knowledge presented in the lectures and available in reference material.

I also think a learning model needs to be communicated to students. Investing some time in the course on discussions of learning, learning how to learn, and the learning model underlying the programme may improve the efficiency of the learning, particularly for students who become 'lost'. The bonus is that a reflective thinking ability is pervasive and leads to improved performance in other aspects of the students' degree programme and life.

I encourage every budding young teacher to videotape his or her efforts in front of the class and in the privacy of a dark room, alone, critically reflect on their effort. My advice to them is to be prepared for some shocks, but the benefits of what they learn from this exercise endure as the initial trauma subsides.

Recently one of my daughters was expressing some frustration towards her course of study and offhandedly remarked, 'I wish my lectures were as good as yours, dad.' This was priceless and a magic moment in my academic career.

REFERENCES

Edwards, J *et al* (1997) *People Rules for Rocket Scientists*, pp 182–85, Samford Research Associates Pty Ltd, Australia

Lord, R A (1998) Engineering wisdom into education, *Journal of Australasian Association for Engineering Education*, **8** (1), pp 45–57

Ramsden, P (1992) *Learning to Teach in Higher Education*, Routledge, London

Ridgway, S and Richiardi, P (1998) Teaching with a passion, *University of Melbourne Gazette*, Autumn, pp 14–15

CHAPTER 6

Just give us the right answer

Case reporter: Brenda Smith

ISSUES RAISED

This case raises the issue of whether a teacher using interactive methods in a lecture should abandon this approach when it seems that little progress is being made towards the desired goal.

BACKGROUND

The case occurs in a large UK university. A female lecturer (an educational developer) has been asked by the engineering department to give a six-hour lecture on developing presentation skills to a group of 80 final-year students. Four weeks later, these students would give individual presentations that are peer assessed.

PART 1

I was daunted by the task. How could I lecture to 80 final-year engineering students for 6 hours and keep them motivated? The request had come at a very busy time in the academic calendar and my mind was certainly on other things. This 'lecturing day' was inconvenient and something that I could do without.

I anticipated that I would face a certain amount of hostility from these engineering students. I could almost hear them saying 'This is not engineering', 'When will we ever need to give a presentation?', 'We will not need this in our future careers', 'This will be boring', 'Will we really have to come back after lunch?', 'Who is this person and what does she know about engineering or presentation skills?'

I knew from the course leader that there would be different cultural groups, including students from Europe and the Far East. I wondered how confident the Far Eastern students would be at giving a presentation in front of their peers. Well I had agreed to give the lecture, so I would make a good job of it even if it was going to be a long day. My plan was to lecture for the first part of the session and then involve the students in interactive group work.

As I walked over to the lecture hall from my office, the sun was shining, which lightened my spirits. I arrived early to set out all the materials and check that 80 chairs had been arranged in tiers of rows in a horseshoe shape in the flat lecture hall I had requested. I chatted to the students as they arrived, trying to learn a few names and to ascertain their views about the course and their career aspirations. The students entered in dribs and drabs, slowly filling the lecture hall. I started on time and the first part of the session went quite well. I talked about the various occasions when giving a presentation would be really useful, trying to give examples that were appropriate to engineering students. Some of the students seemed to show more attention now; maybe this was going to be useful to them after all.

I involved the students as much as possible, drawing examples from them of when they had to give a presentation. They listed features of good and effective presentations. I talked about how important it was to get a good opening, using the expression 'There is no second chance to make a first impression.' I demonstrated how the 'mood' of a presentation could be influenced by playing music. I made use of local artefacts, books or resources such as national costumes as ready-made visual aids. I was trying to include examples from the different cultural groups as well as accommodating students with differing learning styles, such as auditory and visual, hence the music and visual aids. This definitely seemed to be working, as the students were alert and straining to see the examples I was showing. I overheard comments such as 'I would never have thought of using that' and 'What a good idea'.

During the section on body language, I demonstrated how people might interpret different 'strengths' of handshake, how different cultural groups have different comfort zones in terms of body distance and how we can learn a lot about people from observing their gestures. This was a good moment at which to break for lunch. The students left the lecture room looking more cheerful than when they had entered it and I overheard comments such as 'That was interesting', 'Fancy I never realized just how much a handshake can give away'. Maybe this lecture was going to turn out better than I had expected.

I was not looking forward to the after-lunch spot. The students wandered in slowly. Energy was at a low ebb, not helped by the soporific effect of a big lunch and the warm sunny weather. To counter this, I was keen to involve the students in a group activity. In four weeks' time each student would give a 20-minute presentation on his or her project to a group of peers. Their peers would give them feedback against clear agreed criteria that would be designed later in this lecture. It would have been easy to hand out criteria that I had already used elsewhere to assess presentations. However, I wanted to involve the students in an experiential learning process and help them to understand assessment criteria and know how to apply them to their presentations.

The students divided into small groups of no more than 10 and I opened a few windows to keep everyone awake. Students were asked to imagine they were giving their individual presentations and had to decide against what criteria they would like to be assessed. Once criteria were agreed, they were posted on flip chart paper. I circulated around the groups, answering their queries and keeping them task focused. As each group completed the task, they displayed their results. The use of flip chart paper and coloured pens seemed new to the students but they were enthusiastic about the task and seemed particularly keen about posting their work for other groups to see.

To test whether their assessment criteria would work I got the students to apply them to a one-minute presentation given by volunteers. I offered chocolate bars as an incentive to volunteers and they were allowed to choose their topic. The purpose of the one-minute presentation was to give experience and practice in front of their peers, to develop confidence and to apply key learning points from the morning's lecture. But more than this, it would help students to understand the criteria against which they would be assessed in four weeks' time as well as offering them the opportunity to practise giving appropriate feedback to their peers.

Brief feedback was given after each presentation and included two good features and one area for enhancement. There was a pause as each group applied their previously devised criteria. I said we would not discuss the criteria until all the volunteers had presented. The presentations were quite well done and the volunteers especially liked their reward of a chocolate bar. Later presentations were noticeably better than earlier ones as the students applied the peer feedback given earlier. Some real experiential learning was taking place as they saw some of the key issues being demonstrated.

Now all the students had to do was to apply the criteria and agree a final list. Maybe we could all go home early. Everything had been going so well, perhaps too well, because it was then that the crunch came. The students realized that the criteria they had developed in their groups did not work. Some were far too specific, applying only to certain topic areas, while some groups had listed too many detailed criteria. Very few if any of the groups had come up with generic criteria that would apply to a variety of topics. The whole mood of the session changed from one of success to great disappointment and a feeling of failure. A collective sigh could be heard, 'Oh no, after all of this hard work we got it wrong.' All they wanted was for me to give them the 'right answer'. I had some generic schemes for assessing presentations right in front of me. What should I do?

- What do you think the lecturer did next?
- What would you have done in this situation?

PART 2

As usual, I had brought extra material with me – three different coloured sheets of paper, each containing different assessment criteria for presentations. I was very tempted just to give each group a set of these materials and say choose the sheet you think contains the most appropriate criteria. That was the easy answer. That would solve my immediate problem of having to deal with demotivated and frustrated students. However, it was only a short-term solution. I quickly asked myself some hard and searching questions. Do I want them to be critically reflective of their own practice? Yes. Do I really want the students to understand the process of setting fair assessment criteria? Yes. Do I want these students to take on ownership of their criteria? Yes. If I gave them the prepared sets, would they be able to apply the assessment criteria to other situations? Maybe not.

I took a deep breath. I told the students they had made a start and that assessment criteria are not easy to write; that the whole process is developmental and needs time and patience. The task now was to rewrite the original criteria in light of their experience and incorporate possible additional criteria from the coloured sheets. After some moaning and groaning, they settled down to complete the task. Much to my surprise, they soon became engrossed. Again, their work was displayed around the room and groups circulated and added suggestions or helpful comments.

Then came application time. Would their modified set of criteria work? To test this out four stages were followed:

- all groups had 30 minutes to prepare a five-minute presentation;
- three numbers were drawn from a 'hat' to decide which groups presented their work;
- brief oral feedback was given after each presentation;
- presentations were assessed by groups using their modified criteria.

The students approached the task in a mature way and gave helpful and constructive feedback. The quality of the presentations was showing a marked improvement as students' confidence improved. They were listening to their peers and applying feedback. The comments being made were also very supportive and not hostile. Practice was paying off. There was a good feeling of group togetherness and support, and a noticeable improvement in each group's criteria. Was this because they had watched a number of presentations and seen the effect of constructive comments? Was it because they had been given time to practise, reflect, review and modify in light of their experience? I really felt they were beginning to develop their critical thinking skills and demonstrate intellectual maturity.

The final decision now had to be made on which criteria would be selected for the whole group to use with their individual presentations in four weeks' time? Presentation skills were new to the engineering staff, and I had been asked to draw up a list of criteria that the students could use. I had told the students at the beginning of the lecture that they would need to agree on one set of criteria. It would have been easy to select one group or again to 'pull a number out of the hat'. How was I going to ensure all 80 students took on group ownership of the criteria? This was hard going and I was flagging. However, I made an instant decision to get the student groups to negotiate the criteria. I am not sure how the idea came to me. Maybe because they were working so well in groups. There was healthy competition among them, but also group togetherness. They were actually enjoying being part of the decision-making process.

I paired each group with its next nearest group and suggested that everyone contribute to the discussion, that the decision be joint, and not made by the student with the loudest voice. We continued with each large group combining with another group to make two groups of 40. Bedlam followed as each student tried to shout down the next. I stopped everyone and said no consensus was going to be reached by yelling. I suggested each group appoint a spokesperson to negotiate. Within a few minutes, there was agreement on spokespeople for each group. Could two students now negotiate on behalf of their groups and come up with a workable set of criteria for everyone?

Silence reigned; you could hear a pin drop and the tension rose as the two key students sat at a table in the middle of the room. The workings of the United Nations came to mind at this point. Some argument ensued, they protected their 'own patch'. Yet, they knew everyone in the room wanted them to reach a quick and agreeable solution. Within 10 minutes a simple set of five criteria (visual aids, voice, interaction, content and timing) were agreed with marks allocated against each one. You could feel the collective sigh of relief, the sense of elation and the sense of satisfaction.

A final summary of the key points ended the session and they streamed out of the room, talking and laughing. Some stayed behind to talk. 'Why can't other staff use these techniques?', 'That was really useful as I am going for a job interview next week' and 'I now know how difficult it is to write assessment criteria, but I understand what the different criteria now mean.'

In the end, the nervous energy and planning had paid off. I felt the day had been saved because I was able to think on my feet and draw on previous experience. Most importantly, the students left feeling they had achieved success and hopefully their presentations in four weeks' time would demonstrate their newly acquired skills of giving a presentation and being able to reflect and give constructive and helpful feedback to others. All that from one 'lecture'.

- What do you think about the course of action taken by the lecturer? Would you have done things differently?
- Have you experienced a point at which it would be easier to 'give students the answer'? What did you do?
- Could the methods described in this case be used in different settings such as a large, tiered lecture theatre, or in different subject areas? How?

DISCUSSION

This case study raises a number of issues. The first issue concerns one-off lectures. In most cases, one-off lectures are given to an unknown group of students whom the lecturer will not see again. This situation is increasingly common in universities as 'experts' are brought in to deliver a specialized area of the curriculum or practitioners from industry and the professions are used to align the curriculum to the world of work.

In many ways, this is a healthy situation. Lecturers cannot be expert in everything; universities need to ensure relevance and alignment to the outside work and students can benefit from a change of face. However, it is also fraught with potential problems. Although we may know the 'expert' either personally or professionally, we may not know how he or she will perform in front of a diverse group of students. How are 'casuals' and 'experts' inducted into the culture and life of a university? Who is responsible for them and who ensures resources are made available? What happens if they are ineffective and how will we know? What happens if students want additional information or support… to whom do they turn? It is not unknown for part-time staff to say, 'Don't expect to find me outside lecture time as I am only paid to deliver this lecture'! Full-time staff have opportunities to attend staff development workshops that keep them up to date with new learning and teaching initiatives and although these workshops are open to part-time staff, they usually have to attend in their own time. All in all, there is much to think about when we invite or are invited to give a 'one-off' lecture.

A second issue relates to the importance of what are variously called graduate, key, transferable or generic skills. Employers seek graduates who possess skills such as the ability to work in teams, good communication skills and who can 'hit the ground running'. 'There is a widespread recognition that students in higher education should possess a range of key transferable skills in a changing labour market' (AGCAS, 1996). However, 'few students are able to articulate what they have gained from their experience in higher education' (The Association of Graduate Recruiters, 1995). In the UK, the

National Committee of Inquiry into Higher Education (Dearing Report) (1997) emphasized the importance of four key skills: communication, numeracy, use of information technology and learning how to learn. Although universities are coming round to accepting the value of these skills, few staff feel confident to teach them. Many staff came into higher education prepared to teach their subject area but not generic skills and this was evident with the engineering staff. They were certainly supportive of presentation skills being integrated into the curriculum and had already incorporated key skills into their learning outcomes, but they felt they needed support in the teaching of these skills.

In order to encourage students to take presentation skills seriously, staff sometimes make them assessable. The students did indeed take the whole lecture day seriously. They knew they would need to understand the criteria in order to apply them to other students' presentations. It was therefore important for me to support the students in understanding the criteria. Through the process of devising and applying criteria, the students were reviewing their presentation and feedback skills. How often do we ensure that students have time to practise, reflect, discuss and review?

The major issue however, relates to involving the students in their own learning actively – making learning 'real' and experiential. In some ways, it is easy to stand in front of a group of students and deliver the material in a didactic way. The lecturer is in complete control and the material can be delivered in a set time; and on certain occasions, this form of delivery may be appropriate. However the longer the time slot, the more difficult such delivery is to sustain.

According to studies cited in Bonwell and Eison (1991), a lecture begins with a five-minute settling-in period during which students are fairly attentive. This attentiveness extends another five minutes, after which time students become increasingly bored, restless, and confused. Focus and note-taking fall away – some students effectively fall asleep – until the last several minutes of the period when students revive in anticipation of the end of the class. No doubt, the enthusiastic lecturer can extend the time horizon, but actively involving students in their learning is an effective way to keep students' attention and maintain motivation. In the case study I was keen to involve the students early in the day and asked a series of questions on why they thought presentation skills were important to them as a group of future engineers. I involved them in group work where they had to make decisions. I also included other activities such as mini-presentations, devising criteria, negotiating with other groups and giving and receiving feedback, so that students were actively involved and thinking through issues. However, even with all of this activity, it was still very tempting, when things went wrong, to revert to simply 'giving them the answer'. Why did I not do this? Mainly because my experience told me that a way through could be found, that the problem was not insuperable. Teaching in this way can be very physically exhausting for both staff and students, and no more so than when it is necessary to take a risk and enter into an activity from which it is not clear that a successful outcome will emerge. But that is part of the excitement of teaching. Sometimes we will 'get it wrong' and learn from our mistakes, but as in this case, the rewards when we take a chance and see the students thoroughly engaged, are more than worth the risks.

REFERENCES

Association of Graduate Careers Advisory Service (AGCAS) (1996) *Great Expectations: The new diversity of graduate skills and aspirations*, Association of Graduate Careers Advisory Services, Manchester

Association of Graduate Recruiters (1995) *Skills for Graduates in the 21st Century*, Association of Graduate Recruiters, London

Bonwell, C C and Eison, J A (1991) Active Learning: Creating excitement in the classroom, *ASHE-ERIC Higher Education Report No 1*, School of Education and Human Development, George Washington University, Washington, DC

National Committee of Inquiry into Higher Education (1997) *Higher Education in the Learning Society. Report of the National Committee. The Dearing Report*, HMSO, London

CHAPTER 7

PLAYING THE CROWDED HOUSE

Case reporter: Brad Haseman

ISSUES RAISED

This case study raises the issue of the struggle teachers face in trying to enhance teacher–student relationships and address learners' affective needs in a large group lecture situation where students feel remote from the teaching and learning process.

BACKGROUND

The case occurred in the late 1990s when the lecturer took over 'The Arts Today', a first-year course with 300 students and just a single, two-hour lecture once a week. While the male lecturer had taught for over 25 years, 12 in the tertiary setting, he had tended to teach smaller groups in the drama studio and had never lectured to such a large group before.

PART 1

The opportunity to stand in for a highly skilled colleague and teach 'The Arts Today' was more daunting than exciting. Student numbers were large, contact time was small and the content broad – a generalist arts course examining the arts (drama, dance, visual arts and music) across the 20th century. The chances of making a mess of things seemed to be high, although the prospect of working with first-year students was a bright one as I was looking forward to trying to interest them in the world of ideas. So while my colleague began an exotic long-service leave, I was organizing guest lecturers, assembling the book of readings and juggling the half-dozen calls each day asking about the unit, particularly 'What's the assessment like?'

My real concern was that I did not let the subject down. It was widely acknowledged that this unit was a tricky one to coordinate and teach. Some years before I had heard one staff member comment that students thought the subject was 'one of the most reviled courses in the place'! Since then my colleague had worked hard to stabilize the unit by thoughtfully restructuring the content, designing engaging assessment tasks and masterfully using his own impressive lecturing skills. On his return, I did not want him to find the course had re-acquired its 'most reviled' status!

But even before lectures began, I sensed trouble. There were problems with room bookings. The CD ROM material developed especially for the unit had been pressed incorrectly and had to be sent back. Guest lecturers had been tardy in nominating an article to support their lecture, so the book of readings was likely to be late back from the printer. In the countdown to Day 1, students were calling in with all manner of questions; the messages slips and bits of paper were piling up. I was already inundated and lectures had not yet begun.

Then, in the shower of student calls the day before the first lecture, Natalie, one of the students about to start the course, rang. Upset and close to tears, she would not let me politely 'close the call'.

'I need to talk to you. I've bought the book of readings and I can't understand anything. I've tried to read the first article three times but I can't get into it.'

'Well the lecture will help...' I began feebly.

'But I should be able to understand it on my own. I don't think I'll cope at all.'

I tried to assuage her fears. 'I'm sure all will be OK, Natalie. Let's meet after the lecture to discuss things.'

Immediately I obtained a copy of the readings and took them home with me that evening. As I scanned through them, my spirits nosedived. Natalie was right. The readings were hardly pitched for entry-level university students. Some articles were not particularly well written, arguments were overly complex and the concepts tossed around in the discussions would clearly baffle and intimidate many students. In their first reading, they would encounter such notions as 'secular culture', 'polyphonic' and 'paradox' as well as the more obscure 'pseudo-Dionysian', 'a pre-modern Paradise Lost' and 'Miesian minimalism'. I felt as if the unit was unravelling before a word had been uttered. How could I try to clear the conceptual fog that Natalie (and many others, but how many?) would encounter at 9.00 am the next morning?

- What options did the teacher have?
- What would you do if you were in his place?
- How could the teacher communicate individually with each 'Natalie' in the group of 300?

PART 2

I awoke early and in the first light of morning decided to face the problem head on. I went through the first reading once more, compiled a list of the problem concepts and made 300 copies. During the lecture, I distributed the list of terms and raised the problem of unfamiliar terminology and specialist meanings in academic language. I asked the students to mark the terms that were unknown or unclear to them and anonymously return their list to me at the end of the lecture. I made the point that this information would help the guest presenters and I to pitch the lectures at the correct level and be sure to define key terms as we went. In order to control the phone messages I gave out my e-mail address and asked students to contact me that way if they wanted information about any aspect of the subject or if, as one student had already done, they sought clarification of key terms.

After the lecture, I met with Natalie and she seemed reassured by the events of the lecture. She was pleased I had responded to her fears so promptly and now faced the subject with greater confidence. The results from the survey of key concepts were startling, revealing large gaps in the students' knowledge. For instance the following percentages of students declared they did not know the following concepts: secular culture – 37 per cent, polyphonic – 62 per cent, paradox – 65 per cent, pseudo-Dionysian – 59 per cent, a pre-modern Paradise Lost – 49 per cent and Miesian minimalism – 88 per cent. I followed up with the guest lecturers and we discussed ways we would make the conceptual scaffolding of each lecture and reading explicit for the students.

So by the start of the second week the problems raised by Natalie had been addressed and the lectures were under way. I felt confident that all would now be well.

And that is when the problems really began. Opening my e-mail messages the day after the second lecture I found I had around 80 messages – most from students in the 'The Arts Today'. The students had taken me at my word, seeking clarification about every small detail of subject administration and content (details which had often been discussed in the lectures) or taking up my invitation to offer feedback on how they felt the subject was going (even down to a good-natured comment on the tie I wore). And the messages kept coming. Each day I would wearily sit down to a full in-tray but as fast as I would reply to one, another would cheerfully arrive. Clearly, I could not keep this up all semester.

Another alarm bell also began ringing. I was troubled by the general response to the second lecture. The lecture was well organized and illustrated with a couple of telling video extracts but after the first hour the restlessness gradually increased along with the buzz of noise coming from the auditorium. I found this both surprising and irritating. They did not have to come to lectures, so why did they behave in such a rude way, especially as so many had contacted me expressing interest in the subject and concern for their progress. Clearly, the lecture-style delivery with a talking head behind the console at the front of the auditorium did not appear to be able to hold their attention, certainly not for an uninterrupted two hours.

More restless nights. Space now seemed to be the problem. Too much space in the cavernous lecture theatre for a single lecturer to fill and too little administrative space in my schedule to meet the ever-increasing e-mail demands of 300 students. If I felt inundated two weeks earlier, I was now beginning to drown.

- What could the teacher do to manage the e-mail correspondence reasonably but effectively?
- How could the lecturer grab and hold the attention of 300 students for nearly two hours?
- What would you do if you were in the lecturer's place?

PART 3

It was clear that I could not manage the student e-mail demands without help and as the 'new technology' had created this situation, perhaps it could help resolve it. I approached the On-line Teaching Support section of the university to investigate whether 'on-line' technology could make communication between the students and me more manageable but still immediate and personalized. Very quickly they set up a home page for the subject to which we posted all essential information about unit content, structure and assessment. As a query from a student arrived by e-mail, I immediately posted the answer to a Frequently Asked Questions section of the home page for all to see. At the next lecture, I told them that if they had a question they were to check the FAQ section first, before they contacted me, as the answer was likely to be there. As a result, the e-mails dwindled to a trickle of one or two a day. More pleasant and unforeseen surprises followed. The Web-literate students sent in their own useful discoveries, obscure Web sites they had located and books that were particularly helpful. These too were shared (with acknowledgment) on the home page.

I was encouraged by these developments and now felt confident enough to set about energizing the lecture delivery mode. I am not sure why, but I felt the key to this was to redefine the physical space, to break down the invisible line which separated the lecture theatre into the lecturer's space (upfront, beneath the screens and behind the lectern with the control panel for the video, etc) and the student space with its rows of raked seats. A crash course in the use of the lecture theatre meant that for the next week I was able to use a radio microphone, remote controls for CD and video playback and even a remote 'mouse' to control the computer generated visuals. I was no longer chained to the front of the room. Suddenly I could project and assert my presence to and from all parts of the space. Because physical constraints no longer fixed me in a single place, space became a fluid teaching variable. The effect was extraordinary. As I moved freely among the students, there was no longer a single, relentless point of focus for them either. They too were now part of a more dynamic event as I walked among them, addressed them directly or sat beside them while a piece of film played. Immediately the private conversations between students stopped.

With this altered physicality came a re-visioning of the possibilities of the lecture form itself. Together each guest lecturer and I sought to rework the 'taking head' mode of delivery. We realized that with two of us timetabled during the lecture we could turn a monologue from one of us into a dialogue between two of us and between the lectern and the auditorium. The 'other' person could seek clarification, question an assumption, read a piece of text, summarize an argument or directly challenge the presenter. These strategies heightened student engagement especially when the contestations between positions and opinions were robustly (but playfully) argued.

As the semester progressed, we began to harness this playful quality in some quite fresh ways. For example, in the lecture introducing postmodernism, four other teaching staff joined in. The session began traditionally with a lecturer dressed in a suit discussing the importance of the Enlightenment. Gradually, from the auditorium, this discourse was disrupted as the others created a landscape of contesting voices, who, from their multiple speaking positions were able to subvert the authority of the all-knowing academic presenting from the privileged altar of knowledge with parody. By the end of the event, these voices from the margins had defrocked (quite literally as the suit ended scattered around the auditorium) and stripped away the privileged male position.

These experiments led us to develop strategies to 'frame' the students. I would ask them to adopt a particular point of view as they listened to the lecture and so evaluate what was being said according to that point of view. For example, in the lecture considering issues related to 'High and Low Art', students were asked to weigh up two presentations with a quite specific attitude in mind and then make a judgement (allocate funding between the two contesting but worthy bodies) at the conclusion of the lecture. 'Framed' in such a way, students needed to listen with focus and discrimination to identify the aesthetic, economic, social and political issues that imbricated the situation.

The formal student evaluation for this subject was overwhelmingly positive. The home-page facility had effectively addressed the need for all 300 to obtain information about subject requirements in an efficient and friendly way. Many valued its 24-hour accessibility. Many students commented positively at the way students themselves turned the home page into a kind of forum where they would post their own notices and generously support others learning. It was clear too that they valued the way we presented the content of the subject. They enjoyed the challenge of the more complex lecture form and the 'High Art/Low Art' and 'Postmodernism' lectures were both singled out as most engaging.

Since then, I have not had to be so involved with 'The Arts Today'. My colleague returned, refreshed and tanned from leave and took over the reigns once again. However, he has maintained many of the innovations put in place that semester. The home page continues and I contribute to the schedule of lectures. Finally, it was a satisfying experience for me, and continues to be even now, a couple of years later, for I am warmly greeted and occasionally sought out by the now final-year students who have fond memories of 'The Arts Today'.

- Why do you think the students responded so positively to these changes?
- What further options and extensions might be open for the teacher to explore?
- If you had been in the same position, would you have wanted to make such radical changes to the lecture format? Would you have wanted to go further in unsettling the traditional format?

DISCUSSION

There are a number of matters about lecturing in a tertiary setting raised in this case study. One of the most important is that the teacher was prepared to make student concerns and anxieties one of the driving forces in shaping the organization and delivery of the curriculum. Student reaction to the impersonal and faceless teaching which so often characterizes the mass lecture is often negative and resentful as they recognize it can be motivated by the need to 'teach on the cheap'. In his account of events, the teacher places student concerns at the forefront of the teaching process and this shaped his ongoing struggle for improvement. In so doing a strong and workable student–teacher relationship was built up. This case study reminds us once again of the central role that affect plays in learning. Here we find the warmth and strength of the relationship were vital not only for student learning to occur but also to encourage the teacher to take the risks he did. Clearly the students must have been responding positively to these ever-bolder developments and matching the teacher's enthusiasm for transformative change.

As the lecturer began to reshape the lecture form, he was able to draw on a level of personal capacity to perform publicly that may not be shared by all academics. The teacher acknowledged he was more used to working in the drama studio and perhaps this had equipped him with presentational skills which enabled him to 'perform' in these quite transgressive ways. In fact, it is helpful to lay a theatrical frame of reference over these actions; the need to heighten the 'watchability' of the event draws its impulse from the central challenge facing all playwrights, directors and actors. The move to shift the students away from being a monolithic and passive audience attending a lecture, towards actively implicating them in what is being presented (as in the 'High Art/Low Art' lecture) has much in common with notions of audience participation and interactivity in contemporary performance.

In fact, one of the most important lessons that can be drawn from this case study is the sense of personal pleasure and excitement that saturates the teacher's account of the subject's evolution. As teachers, our own creative impulses are necessary to keep the teaching transaction fresh and vital. This teacher admits he did not really know why he felt the need to redefine the space of the lecture theatre, but certainly it had a major impact on the subsequent teaching and learning process. This intuitive and creative questing for solutions is a characteristic of all effective teaching, yet so often the conventional lecture mode denies the innovative or intuitive, insisting on predictable patterns of delivery for well-known and stable content. But there are no sensible grounds for this. Indeed, if masses of students are to have more than a faceless experience in the crowded houses of our universities, then academics need to bring all their creative passion, playfulness and willingness for risk into the lecture theatre with them.

QUESTIONS FOR PERSONAL REFLECTION

- What mechanisms do you have for gathering ongoing feedback from students on the effectiveness of your lecturing? How do you use that feedback and do the students know you use it?
- How do you manage the heavy administrative loads that accompany large group coordination in ways that are efficient but also develop positive relationships with your students?
- The flexibility in teaching outlined in this case study depends upon staff working together to plan their presentations. What factors enhance or inhibit such collaboration?
- Are there any aspects of the form of your current lectures that you may consider altering as a result of the approach outlined in this case study?

CHAPTER 8

WE MIGHT HAVE TO LEARN IT BUT WE SHOULDN'T HAVE TO THINK ABOUT IT

Case reporter: Lorraine Stefani

ISSUES RAISED

This case study raises issues of teaching sensitive course content and of ensuring inclusiveness in large classes.

BACKGROUND

The events of this case occurred in a university in Northern Ireland. A 38-year-old female with eight years' experience teaching is lecturing on the prenatal diagnosis of genetic disorders. There are 80 students in the class, about equal numbers of men and women, mainly 18–19 years old.

PART 1

When I started teaching, my methods were based very much on how I had been taught as a student. My lectures were of the formal transmission of delivery style with me in the driving seat and the students interested passengers. At least that is how I have now come to think of my early teaching experiences. However, on marking examination papers that invariably involved reading my own lecture outpourings, I came to consider that there must be other ways of teaching that would result in deeper learning than this. I taught human genetics and was always concerned that the students viewed the issues of genetic diagnosis in a very two-dimensional manner, did not grasp that topics such as prenatal diagnosis of genetic disorders might well apply to them and that this was not just a textbook issue.

I started to wonder if I could find a way of teaching the subject that would make the issues more alive and immediate. I devised a teaching method that I thought would bring the human aspect of the subject to the fore as a way of trying to enhance student learning and independent thought. With a colleague, I devised a card game that involved students working in pairs and engaging in a role play. Cards were given out to the student pairs that detailed the status of each pair for the gene responsible for cystic fibrosis, Huntington's chorea or Duchenne muscular dystrophy. The idea was that the partnership would then examine their gene status and work out the risk of having a child born with any of these three particular genetic disorders.

The pairs discussed what options they might pursue, such as whether the best thing to do is not have children, to ask for prenatal diagnosis using the new sophisticated DNA diagnostic probes (that had been discussed in previous lectures) or not to consider the risk of having a child with a genetic disorder as an issue at all. The partnerships were then asked to consider the dilemmas that may be associated with the concept of termination of pregnancy.

To include this 'game' and 'role play' as part of a lecture I made sure I could get a flat room to work in so that students could move around more easily than in a tiered lecture theatre. The first time I used this method it was very successful. Students valued seeing the issues in terms that are more personal. They said in evaluation forms this had made them think more seriously about the long-term ethical issues associated with the Human Genome Project and some of them also said that it was the first time they had actually heard their peers' views on controversial issues. The class was very animated and there was a great buzz in the lecture room, so much so that a colleague looked in the door to check that everything was all right. Students told me afterwards that they had talked to family members about the topics and that they now had a much better understanding of the implications of genetic disorders and diagnosis. I was very pleased with the level of discussion and debate occurring between the students and I felt that it would be good to use this method of teaching again.

The second time I was preparing to use this teaching method, it so happened that one of the students who would be in the class actually had cystic fibrosis. A colleague had introduced me to Sarah, one of his tutees who was pursuing a course in science education and who wanted to talk to me about my human genetics course. Sarah said that she had a strong interest in the isolation of the cystic fibrosis gene from the point of view of the possibility of a cure. Because of the course Sarah was pursuing, she was choosing human genetics as an optional module and so did not initially know the rest of the students in the class but she was happy that she would meet new students.

I talked Sarah through what I would be doing in class, including the card game and role play and asked Sarah if she felt all right about that. I was aware of the sensitivities that surround the issue of prenatal diagnosis and discussing the possibility of termination of pregnancy if any genetic disorders are apparent. I had not, however, experienced having anyone with a clearly defined genetic disorder in my class when encouraging discussion and debate. So I wanted at least to try to determine whether Sarah would find the subject matter and the teaching method difficult to cope with.

Sarah was very happy to join in discussions and debate and was looking forward to the course. I was very happy when it came round to time for the role-play session, looking forward to the buzz that is around when students are interacting and engaging with difficult issues. I mused as to whether I should not do all my teaching in this way or at least find ways of turning lectures into more active sessions.

In this next class, the role play provoked plenty of discussion, but it was clear to me that not all partnerships had worked well. In order to encourage student interaction I kept an eye on the body language between student pairs or groups, hovering when the students were working to tune into their discussions and to share ideas. One or two male students refused to engage in the role play for reasons of their religion. For them prenatal diagnosis was not an issue; it just would not be considered. I had thought about Sarah, but I had not really thought about other students considering the issues to be out of bounds for discussion for other reasons such as religion. I was pondering all of this when another student John, who in general is good humoured, has plenty of potential and does not take himself too seriously, said to the whole class:

> This is an OK exercise. But really, I can't see what all the fuss is about. A foetus is nothing more than a bundle of cells. Nobody in their right mind would want to deliberately have a 'handicapped' child. I think the Pope is out of touch with reality.

'Oh dear!' I thought. 'This is NOT good. How am I going to handle this?' But as the students looked towards me I was under no illusion that it was up to me to respond. Some students were outraged and started shouting at one another across the class. The pertinent issues were of course lost in the shouting and confusion and the class was turning into a rabble. Sarah looked quite upset. John, on the other hand, looked quite pleased to have caused such a stir.

- Do you think what happened should have been avoided? If so, how?
- What would you have done if confronted by this situation?
- What do you think the teacher actually did do?

PART 2

I took a deep breath, and said, 'I think we'll bring this aspect of the debate to an end and focus on wider ethical issues surrounding the isolation of and use of gene probes.' I then took back charge of the class by presenting some of the issues and suggesting the class think about them for the next lecture session.

I was glad to finish the session to get back to my office and think about it all. I was slightly shocked and thought I had probably upset the sensitivities of many students. I was not surprised that the session was the subject of much discussion amongst the students. I tended to hear such feedback from the colleague with whom I shared an office. This feedback was usually given in a subtly negative form as 'trendy' teaching techniques were not encouraged in the department, and a perceived failure affirmed this stance. 'Trendy learning' was not too popular either. Some students reported to other staff, 'We might need to learn about gene probes and prenatal diagnosis but we shouldn't have to think about them.'

I faced criticism from some of my colleagues that occurred either directly within my shared office or indirectly through 'banter' in the tea room. Some of the 'banter' was about using 'trendy' teaching techniques that students were not ready for. Some of it had a level of gender bias that made me question whether I was trying to impose views on the students through the card game and role play. Indeed, many of my male colleagues seemed to enjoy insinuating that I was manipulating students with my feminist views. 'Would it not be wiser to use the conventional lecture format and avoid personal discussion of controversial topics?' was one comment. Another colleague suggested that discussing ethical issues was unnecessary. I found all of this unnerving. Because the staff were conservative and mainly male, most of what my male colleagues had to say went unchallenged and I was not actually particularly sure I would have the support of the other women. And at this time I did not have the pedagogical knowledge to support my arguments for innovative approaches to teaching.

I was quite concerned about Sarah and how she felt about the implications of the discussions. I talked to the colleague who had introduced me and said to mention to Sarah that if she wanted to have a chat about that last class just to drop in on me. Sarah did come and although understandably she had felt a bit upset, she did feel that people have different views and that it was good to hear the views of other students. She felt more upset at the way in which the class had become aggressive and thought it was terrible that some students were so intolerant of the views of others. Sarah felt fine about continuing with the course.

I was also curious to know if John had deliberately shifted the tenor of the class by being so provocative. Essentially, I felt that although he had created a storm, he was only expressing an opinion. I also thought more about the context of the discussion and the emotions associated with both religion and abortion in Northern Ireland. I decided to have an informal conversation with John to find out more. John was an amiable student, and very keen, but did not take himself too seriously. He told me, 'I just wanted to create a stir and get the students talking because generally they are so uncommunicative in class. I suppose I might have been a bit more careful about what I said.' I asked him if he knew that one of the students in the class has cystic fibrosis. He had not known and consequently felt a bit mortified by what he had said.

The next time I took the class, passions had ebbed. There was no obvious sign of lasting upset but I did not want to revisit the controversies, so I did not review the last class but immediately moved on to the next topic. I had no answer to the colleagues who criticized both my teaching methods and content (despite the fact that course content was always discussed and approved at staff committees), so I chose not to mount a defence. In my teaching, I had enthusiasm for actively involving students but I had no peda-gogical underpinning for this. I was teaching in an instinctive manner which was different from my colleagues but I did not have a theoretical under-standing of teaching and learning to justify my methods, so I did not want to rock the boat. This was a learning experience for me that I would have to build on. I felt I could take my time and not be too revolutionary! I would have to think carefully about structuring my lectures so that I could encourage discussion but be prepared for the unexpected or at least be aware that the unexpected can occur when you give students more freedom of expression.

Other issues also troubled me and gave plenty of scope for reflection. Sometimes I thought 'Should I bother trying to relate important scientific topics to potential real-life situations?' Was this necessarily fair on the students? I was concerned that my teaching method left scope for students to make comments with which I did not necessarily agree or disagree but which were maybe offensive to other students on religious, political, health, or disability grounds. I began to appreciate the complexities and dilemmas associated with 'good teaching'.

I did not want to court controversy in this way again because it was so stressful. In later classes I dealt with the potentially controversial issues very differently, using videos and mini-case studies. I did not revert to a totally transmission mode of teaching again, but for a period of time I kept more 'control' of classes.

- Have you experienced a similar situation in your own classes? If so, how did you handle it?
- What responsibility does a teacher have to debrief with students after a controversial episode?
- Is it possible for students to 'learn without thinking', as suggested by one of the students?

DISCUSSION

This case centres on my attempts to manage the 'facilitation of active learning' in a large class in the context of a lecture. It is about taking the risk

of giving students freedom to express their views and opinions on controversial topics. From the outset, I was quite confident of using the card
game/role play in class. It had been successful before, it got students talking
and I had seen more thoughtful exam essays on the topic using this method
than I had previously. With the benefit of hindsight and a great deal more
knowledge and understanding of pedagogical principles, I might have
considered doing some preparatory work with the class before using the
game. For example, I could have flagged the course and lecture content and
methods at the beginning of the series of lectures and asked how students felt
about these issues. This would have allowed sensitive topics to be aired and
discussed in a more controlled environment. Much as I had done with Sarah,
I could have given an outline of the session before presentation of the card
game/role-play exercise, sensitized students to the emotional potential of the
topic and perhaps attempted to establish some ground rules. I might even
have created the potential to opt out of the role play by introducing an
'either/or' option – either work in pairs on the card game or work on a series
of genetic diagnosis problems.

However, that raises an important issue, that if a topic is controversial, as
mine was, does that mean students can simply 'opt out'? It also raises a fundamental question about the nature of a university – that is, is the notion of
open and rational debate a core value, or something you can take or leave
depending on your opinion? My own view is that open and rational debate is
very often uncomfortable, but so too is most transformative learning. We do
not necessarily insist on students thinking in a particular way, but we DO
insist on them thinking. That was what I was trying to do in this situation.

Northern Ireland has a large number of Catholics who are against abortion
on principle and additionally many fundamental/conservative Protestants are
also opposed to abortion. So, given that abortion was and is a highly sensitive
topic, I could have anticipated that religion and politics might become
entangled in the subject matter I was teaching.

I could have considered more deeply the potential for discussion about
prenatal diagnosis and selective abortion to be upsetting for Sarah and
thought about whether I still wanted to run the class this way. An alternative
would be to develop other ways of teaching that would engage the students
but not require them to express their views publicly, or even not to raise the
issue at all. This raises questions for me about how 'inclusive' our teaching
methods should be. Can 'inclusive teaching' encompass individual sensitivities when teachers are dealing with diversity in large classes? I made time to
talk to Sarah before and after the lecture. It is equally possible to envisage that
there were students with both seen and unseen disabilities in my class. There
are increasingly large and diverse classes in higher education comprising
students at different levels of maturity, students entering higher education
through alternative pathways, and students with very different cultural and
educational backgrounds. These combine to produce very real tensions

around the concept of 'inclusive teaching'. Is it possible for individual lecturers in large classes to meet the learning needs of all of their students and to anticipate students' views? Is it better to take some risks and be innovative or to resort to safe ground always? However I would not argue that diversity should mean censorship, but rather that the coming together of alternative views and backgrounds is 'refereed' in a sensitive, supportive and fair manner.

I was taken aback by John's behaviour and the subsequent classroom rabble. My way out of it was to reorganize the class and move on to a wider topic. I did not really have the confidence to take hold of the arguments and turn them into a more rational and constructive discussion. This could be considered a missed opportunity given that the reason for introducing innovative teaching techniques was to encourage students to engage with difficult and controversial topics. It takes courage to turn around a conflict situation and I was not sure I could do that. If I had had the confidence and the courage, I might have succeeded in persuading the students to think more deeply, to justify their own comments and arguments and put them forward in a rational way. On the other hand, I might have exacerbated the situation. If something similar happened now I would ride the storm and I would feel more confident about asking students to justify their comments for example. I would ask for clarification quietly and rationally so that all could understand what is being said and why. This does not mean that they would all have to agree, but they would have to engage to understand and to be able to say why they disagree. But I am also more careful now about discussing my teaching methods and strategies with students, although I am aware that good teachers learn to take chances and learn from what works and what does not.

Although John's comments were highly controversial to some students, it was not the comments themselves that upset me but rather the consequences of his comments that left me feeling out of control. Many of the students were clearly not happy. I had no real mechanism for addressing this in any overt way, so I did my best to maintain good rapport with the students and moved on to new topics. I still think of this as a reasonable action because I cannot be held responsible for students' views. However, I was responsible for setting the stage upon which those views were aired. By getting involved in the arguments, I might have begun to impose my own views inadvertently, or was I seeking clarification and alternative arguments, rather than imposing my own view? Controversial topics will arise across different subject areas and however they are taught lecturers and teachers should try to be neutral, see that both sides of an argument are fairly put and not impose their own politics. It is, however, important to 'air' rather than 'avoid' controversial matters.

There is, however, another general issue relating to teachers' knowledge about the students in their classes. If 'inclusive teaching' is a goal for higher education, then teachers, tutors and lecturers need to know about the students we are teaching. Such knowledge will influence our attitudes and the teaching methods we use. However, that will not necessarily affect how students behave if they do not know anything about their fellow students. This could pose some teaching and learning dilemmas for us. There is much focus on teaching in a manner that is considered to be 'inclusive'. In order to create safe space for learning perhaps we should be paying more attention to enabling students to develop essential skills such as critical thinking, developing and presenting an argument and encouraging tolerance towards difference and different views. We need to produce learning environments where these skills can be safely learned and developed and with ground rules for this to take place.

In the years following this incident, I developed a positive reputation for being an innovative teacher, presented some of my teaching developments at conferences and published my work. However, this one particular incident had a very powerful effect in making me think through the appropriateness of the teaching methods that I use in this and my other classes.

QUESTIONS FOR PERSONAL REFLECTION

- Do you have any way of knowing the level of student diversity in the classes you teach, eg racial issues, disability, religion, etc?
- How do you respond to diversity in your classes?
- How do you approach controversial topics in the classroom?

PART 3

DEALING WITH FEEDBACK

CHAPTER 9

GETTING TO KNOW YOU

Case reporter: Mark Griffiths

ISSUES RAISED

The central issue raised by this case is how to make content material relevant and interesting to students.

BACKGROUND

This case took place at a large UK university. A young lecturer at the start of his academic career is required to teach applied psychology in a range of professional courses. He has little experience in lecturing and little knowledge of the professional areas of his students. Both he and his students see little relevance in the material he is required to teach.

PART 1

I got my first full-time lecturing post back in September 1990 when I managed to secure a one-year temporary lectureship in a department of psychology. At the time of the appointment I was 23 years old, still finishing my PhD, and had never been given formal advice or guidance on how to teach. I soon realized I had been dropped in at the deep end. In essence, my job was to 'plug the teaching gaps' and I was given a whole range of duties, including the teaching of developmental psychology to various nursing groups, social psychology to police inspectors and health psychology to podiatrists.

I felt totally out of my depth as I prepared lecture after lecture for student groups with whom I had little or no affinity. The students in these groups were typically mature age and it was common for me to be the youngest person in the room – by 20 years. I had a lot of trouble relating to the students. They were quite often part-time students who came in for one day a week. They found it hard to appreciate the relevance of psychology to their studies. I have to admit that I sometimes found it hard to see the relevance too!

One course in particular was a headache. Every Wednesday morning I taught psychology to podiatry students on a newly validated BSc Podiatry course. I did not even know what Podiatry was! I ended up teaching health psychology to students who became demotivated because of the situation they found themselves in. Also they were only sitting my modules as a means to an end (ie to get their degree). Neither the students nor I could see the relevance of what I was teaching. I really did not know what to do to make it better for both my students and me. In addition to this, my modules were ridiculed by other staff members. Colleagues would have a laugh at my expense, saying things like 'How was FEET 101 today?' and 'Did they find your jokes corny?'

The critical incident occurred at the end of my first year of teaching when I received formal written feedback from the students. Although they had no problem with my lecturing style, they found what I had to say totally irrelevant to their studies. The word 'irrelevant' rang in my ears for weeks. Knowing I was going to be teaching them next year meant I had to do something to address the situation for the following academic year. I could not cope with that kind of feedback again.

- What would you do in this situation?
- What do you think Mark actually did?

PART 2

Discussing the outcomes of the feedback with the students, I realized that I lacked not only knowledge about podiatry but also about teaching and how to deliver material effectively to the students. Although I felt rejected, I knew that I wanted to improve the situation on both counts.

The solution came from an unexpected quarter – the university's own teacher-training course. At the start of my second year of lecturing, I was told that I must attend the university teacher-training course. I was told by my head of department that this was for my own personal development as much as to get formal teacher-training experience. Fortuitously, the teacher-training course started a month or so before my lecturing and I got many suggestions from colleagues about how to solve the problems that I had. An underlying theme to many of the suggestions involved 'getting to know the students better'. I had never learnt the names of the students in my groups (as I only saw them briefly once a week). I never saw any of them in their work context and to be honest I never even knew what they actually did in their clinical setting. I never engaged in any social interaction after the lectures were over (I just wanted to get out as quickly as possible) and I never interacted with other staff members on the podiatry degree.

I decided that the only way to get myself out of the rut I was in and gain the students' trust was to start interacting with them both inside and outside of the classroom. I did this in a number of ways:

- I learnt the students' names.
  At the end of my first session at the start of my second year, I took home a set of student photographs and learned the names of everyone in the class. Thankfully, there are no more than about 25 students per year on the course. In the second session, the students were totally amazed that I knew all their names. The fact that I had taken the effort to familiarize myself with everyone on the course at some level appeared to pay dividends!
- I sat in on student clinics.
  I asked the School of Podiatry if I could start sitting in on student clinics. This gave me a good insight into what the students did on a day-to-day basis. Not only could I incorporate real examples into the lectures but also students began to realize I did care about what they were doing and realized I wanted to make my teaching relevant.
- I 'joined' the podiatry staff.
  I asked for my own pigeonhole in the School of Podiatry and began to spend time in the Podiatry staffroom and talk to other members of the degree staff. This changed my status as an 'outsider' and both podiatry staff and students started to see me as a bona fide member of the podiatry staff.
- I socialized with the students out of class.
  Every Wednesday I would go to the pub or canteen where the podiatry students ate lunch and would chat with them informally about how I could improve my modules and what they would like to see introduced. This proved much better as a feedback mechanism than survey forms. As a consequence, I started to be invited out to student social occasions such as the Christmas Dinner and the end of year post-results parties.
- I researched and published in their professional area.
  I started to do psychological research within the podiatric setting with other staff members. I also started to publish things in outlets such as *The Journal of British Podiatric Medicine* or refer to my podiatry groups in other writings. For instance, a 'Don's Diary' that I wrote for the *Times Higher Educational Supplement* was displayed by students with pride on their noticeboard because I had mentioned them!

It is hard to assess which of these was the most important in getting the students on my side since there was an overall accumulative effect. However, my regular presence at the clinics (at least at the start of the year) was noticed by all the students and they saw this as an important step in me getting to know what they were all about. I also began to appreciate why some of my previous teaching was totally irrelevant having seen them in action. In essence, my actions were not just concerned with getting students on my side but were also about using a range of academic methods to help me understand the students and the material I had to teach.

QUESTIONS FOR PERSONAL REFLECTION

- How well do you think Mark handled the situation?
- Have you ever had to teach a group that you felt you had little or no affinity with? How did you deal with the situation?
- Do the issues raised in this have relevance for any particular areas in your current teaching?

DISCUSSION

In retrospect, perhaps being thrown in at the deep end did me more good than harm because it meant I had to learn quickly from my mistakes. However, this kind of approach certainly would not suit everyone and I think it was only my resilience and desire to make it as a lecturer that got me through those first 12 months.

One of the underlying themes of this case study concerns the utility of applying a particular subject (eg health psychology) to a professional service area (eg podiatry). Lecturers need to think very carefully about how they relate their material in these instances. For some areas, there is little established history. For instance, the introduction of a psychology component into podiatry courses is a recent innovation that has only come in during the last decade or so in the UK. I taught psychology to trainee podiatrists for five years. I believe that psychology has relevance to most aspects of our lives and therefore must be relevant within a podiatry training programme. The main objective of such training is to produce an individual who is not only competent in relevant clinical skills but has also gained the interpersonal skills which will enable them to care more effectively for their patients.

The most important thing a lecturer must do when teaching his or her subject to a particular profession is acquire knowledge about what that group of people do on a day-to-day basis and the conditions in which they do it. Without this knowledge, it is almost impossible to design a course that will be relevant to the group's specific needs. My own knowledge acquisition of podiatry evolved slowly utilizing information obtained from my students in combination with direct observations of my students working in the clinical setting. It was the time I initially spent in the clinic that helped me most in teaching psychology to the podiatrists. This was particularly helpful in allowing me to give relevant examples. The students also began to realize that I wanted psychology to have an impact on them and I started to discuss with them the potential applications.

The problem I had with podiatry is also played out in other situations and it is possible to learn from these. For example, there are parallels with psychology courses for nurses and for medical students. However, it would be unwise to use these as a foundation on which to build a course since there are enormous differences between the paramedical professions. For example, podiatry is different in terms of the 'patient–carer' relationship to that in nursing, where (in general) more time is spent with individual patients in single meetings and over protracted periods. The trick then is to learn what we can from similar contexts, but to also take the time to find out about the particular teaching circumstance in which we find ourselves.

Another underlying theme of this case is preparing and supporting new lecturers in their role. My attendance on the teacher-training course was without doubt a major turning point in my career development and is some-thing that I believe should be compulsory for all new lecturers. Not only was I given suggestions and advice on how to solve my problem but I also gained valuable support from my peers. I also found that I could give something back to the others on the course. This peer support was something I had not really experienced during my first-year lecturing because I felt so out of touch with all the members of my department. I think this was partly due to age, since I was 13 years younger than the next youngest member of staff, and there was nobody I felt I could share my troubles with. On the teacher-training course, I was surrounded by people who had the same or similar experiences as me.

Negative feedback has led me to think about learning and teaching issues. But at the time it was painful and isolating. For some people, negative feedback on modules they teach is all par for the course. For a new lecturer, negative feedback can be psychologically devastating. It can affect your self-esteem. It makes you question whether you will ever 'cut it' as a lecturer and you wonder whether you have made the right career choice. In short, those new to lecturing may have neither coping strategies to deal with student rejection, nor compar-isons from which to interpret the feedback more objectively.

While it may be that much of this case study is common sense, it is inter-esting to see how often lecturers fail to connect their students to the subject matter because they themselves have failed to understand the problem. It can be easier to blame the students or the curriculum than to investigate, learn and change. I could not change the curriculum – that was predetermined, so essentially I stayed with the same content but gave examples that are more relevant. In addition, I did not have to modify my teaching style, as I received positive comments from the students, and therefore my style was not in question. However, any taught module in an intensive vocational course must contribute in a relevant, productive and appropriate way. This has to be the responsibility of the lecturer and he or she must do as much background research as possible to facilitate the process. In addition, this one experience in teaching podiatry has been transferred to all areas of my teaching.

CHAPTER 10

Is it me?

Case reporters: Helen Whiffen and Patricia Kalivoda

ISSUES RAISED

This case focuses on the issues of a personal style in lecturing, the questions raised by negative feedback from students, and the use that can be made of such feedback to improve the students' learning environment.

BACKGROUND

The case is about Mackenzie, a 30-year-old assistant professor who had been teaching for one semester in the School of Forestry at a research university in the south-eastern United States when these events took place. She was asked to design and teach a required computing course called Spatial Data and Analysis to undergraduate junior forestry students. The students preferred to work outdoors rather than inside in front of a computer.

PART 1

I was excited yet nervous about teaching this new course in a forestry programme, as I had been planning it for many months. The course was required of students in all four majors offered in the forestry programme. There was, however, no standardized curriculum for the course, which was a new field in forestry. The course I designed was innovative and based, as much as possible, on real-world scenarios that the students would find in the workplace. Owing to the nature of the course content, I thought the students would be highly motivated and keen to do well. I therefore looked forward with eager anticipation to my first semester teaching the course.

Graduates from forestry programmes obtain jobs in a wide variety of organizations from forest resource organizations, both private and public, to research and service programmes concerned with the advancement of forestry both locally and globally. This new course covered the use of computer-based spatial data to help integrate in-the-field forestry practices.

Before I arrived, the course was scheduled to be lecture-based with a 3-hour laboratory component. For my lectures, I prepared PowerPoint slides to be displayed via a projection system, in a large 100-chair auditorium. Class enrolment was expected to run at between 35 and 50 students per semester.

Personally, I prefer a question-and-answer type dialogue to a straight didactic lecture format. A question-and-answer format helps me monitor where students are having trouble with the material. To involve the students further, I ask students to complete a self-organized seating chart showing me where each student sits, so I can memorize their names and therefore address them personally when asking questions in class. I feel it is important to get to know the students; I want to develop a good relationship with them. Being able to call them by their first name helps.

When introducing a new concept in a lecture, I try to model the problem-solving process. I give an example of how the concept is used, followed by a second example with a question-and-answer dialogue. For example, one of the first topics I cover in the class is spatial data structure: how computer software keeps track of the location of spatial objects in virtual space. This is a fundamental concept for students learning about spatial data. If students understand data structure, they can understand data development when they start making their own data.

One type of data structure is linear data. When I introduce the structure of linear data, we discuss examples of the kinds of spatial objects that are represented by lines in forested areas, such as streams and power lines. Next, we review the new terminology. Each part of the structure has a specific name. Using a basic coordinate system with x- and y-axes, I explain about the starting and ending points of lines (nodes), the directional changes along lines (vertices), and the sides of lines (left polygon, right polygon). For each part, I use an actual attribute table to show how the computer keeps track of each 'nut or bolt', along with an illustration of the spatial object that 'grows' in complexity throughout the lecture.

Next, I present a new example and call on students, asking them to walk the whole class through each step of the problem-solving process verbally. For example, starting with a fresh illustration, I will call on Fred to explain to the class:

- how many nodes are required to 'hold the data in place';
- where must the nodes be located;
- how will each node be recorded in an attribute table?

I will then call on Sarah to locate the required vertices. We continue through the example until the attribute table is complete and the spatial object is firmly located in space.

During the first semester that I taught this course, it appeared that the students were able to use the new terminology appropriately. During the class example, they accurately recorded the locations of the nodes and vertices in the attribute table. With little coaching, each student called upon was able to answer the question posed. If one student suggested the placement of a node where others thought it unnecessary, we discussed the logic the student had used to arrive at his/her answer. The students contributed well to the discussion.

The laboratory exercise that corresponded with this lecture required the students to use, outside of class, the problem-solving process presented in class. The students were to pretend that they were computer software and generate the attribute tables like spatial software for a given figure. The lab exercise was designed to walk the students, step-by-step, through the process, identifying the locations of the required nodes and vertices, and recording these locations on the blank attribute table provided.

During my first semester, my concerns about the class began when I walked into the lecture hall the day before this lab assignment was due. I could feel the students' frustration. They immediately started complaining. Bonnie expressed confusion over how to complete the attribute tables. Steven confessed that he could not distinguish the functional difference between a node and a vertex. Tracy was concerned that the x- and y-coordinates of her nodes and vertices did not exactly match the locations recorded by her friend Becky. Tommy wanted to know why Bruce had six more vertices listed in his attribute table than he did, and both Tommy and Bruce wanted to know who was 'right'.

I could see the students were getting upset. They had successfully completed the process in class, but they were finding it difficult to apply the process to a new problem. It was obvious from their faces that they had decided that this course was going to be very difficult.

I, too, was frustrated. It seemed like the students were stringently avoiding any opportunity to think independently. I became distressed. In my past teaching experiences as a graduate teaching assistant and as an extension specialist, I had been repeatedly commended for being able to simplify concepts by using down-to-earth examples. This display of student frustration and confusion was new to me and very unsettling.

- What should Mackenzie do next?
- What would you do in the same situation?

PART 2

I decided to find out directly from the students why they were unhappy with the course. I knew this would be a time-consuming and difficult thing to do if I was to attempt it by myself. After all, I had only been teaching one semester. I needed some support. I applied for, and was selected, to participate in a two-year faculty development programme designed for junior faculty members. As part of the programme, I received a small instructional improvement grant. For my project, I designed a classroom research project comprised of three parts:

- a peer consultation with a senior faculty member;
- a written survey to be completed by all the students in the class;
- focus group interviews to be conducted with a small number of the students in the class.

The first part of the classroom research project was to solicit feedback from an outside observer. I contacted the institution's Office of Instructional Support and Development and asked to be assigned a peer mentor. They matched me with Debbie, a senior faculty member in the College of Education.

Debbie and I had our first meeting over lunch at a local deli. I sincerely enjoyed our conversation. Debbie seemed genuinely interested in my concerns about the course and she had many good ideas about classroom strategies. Debbie observed six of my lectures. We met after each observation and she provided me with a number of suggestions. Over the semester, I experimented with a number of her suggested strategies. Debbie monitored my progress by continuing to observe some of my lectures.

The second part of my classroom research project was to design a written survey instrument that was administered to all of the students in my class over a two-semester period. The third part of the project was to hire a graduate student well versed in qualitative methodology to design and administer anonymous, individual 45-minute interviews with six of the students from the course.

I felt somewhat apprehensive about what I might learn from the survey instrument and interviews. I was glad that I was working under the direction and with the support of expert professionals.

- What do you think will be the major issues identified by the students?
- How do you think Mackenzie will react?

PART 3

Some of the students' answers to the questions in the written survey stunned me. First, I was surprised to find that, in response to a general question I asked regarding the attributes of a good course, the students consistently indicated as crucial the following two attributes:

- a high level of professional experience by the teacher as perceived by the students;
- a high level of respect for the teacher from colleagues as perceived by the students.

In terms of my course in particular, they resented that it was compulsory, that there was a lot of material to cover, and that there were no opportunities for outside lab work. Further, they were less than thrilled with the high level of computer use in the course and the lack of adequate computer support within the department.

- What do you think Mackenzie will do next?
- If you were in Mackenzie's position, how would you deal with the students' feedback?

PART 4

Up to this point I had always thought that a good teacher was someone who knew the subject matter, was enthusiastic about the subject matter, was intent on helping the students 'get' the subject matter, was respectful of the students, produced interesting opportunities for learning (experimentation), was fair, and was organized. I felt that I had applied each of these principles to the course. And yet, something was missing. Through this project, I discovered that my personality traits and teaching style were negatively affecting the students' approach to the course.

By engaging in the classroom-research project, I began to understand the perceptions of the students. The challenge was to develop strategies to address the students' perceptions about me, as an individual and a faculty member, and about the course content. So, how could I best use the feedback I had been given to improve the students' learning environment?

I decided to begin by working on my presentation style. I asked my peer mentor, Debbie and a colleague in the Office of Instructional Support and Development, Claire, to help me. Exposing my concerns to these colleagues was easy. I was hungry to talk with people who were interested and could shed some light on the situation. I felt I could be completely candid with them because they were tenured faculty members outside the forestry programme.

At their suggestion, I:

- mingled informally with students before class;
- slowed down the pace of the lectures by slowing the rate of my speech and pausing frequently to give students time to catch up on their note taking;

- produced a packet of notes that contained all of the lecture slides so that students did not have to take as many notes verbatim;
- moved around the lecture hall while lecturing, using a laser pointer to focus student attention on particular aspects of a slide on the screen;
- let students use the laser pointer to point to areas on the slides to get them physically involved in the question they were asking or the answer they were providing.

It is still too early to say whether these changes are having a significant effect on my relationships with students in the class. However, based on the input from Debbie and Claire, I believe that I am making the best effort possible.

DISCUSSION

This case study raises a number of issues. The first relates to teaching style and the attributes of an effective teacher. Lecturing is a complex activity, and it involves one's own personal style. Some lecturers put a premium on the interaction with students through questions, discussions and other activities. Others favour a predominantly oral style of lecturing, with comparatively little use of an overhead projector or PowerPoint slides. Equally, some see lectures as a powerful means of stimulating and motivating students to think.

I thought I knew what made a teacher effective, and I applied my set of principles to the course. I was enthusiastic about the subject matter, I wanted to share the subject with others and I had put in many hours of preparation time and was well prepared. Yet, it is important to keep in mind that while both teaching style and techniques are important, the key focus must always be on effective student learning. Through this project I realized that something related to me was missing.

I am a relatively young female from another part of the United States teaching in a male-dominated field in the south-eastern United States. I like efficiency and organization. In a lecture, I focus on the concepts and the critical thinking skills needed to make decisions. These are the things that matter. These are the reasons we are in class. It is the message that matters; the messenger is irrelevant, no?

I have no experience telling stories or describing past work experiences in such a tantalizing manner as to grab the listener's ear. I provide the relevant facts in a very bare bones conversational style. I, by nature, talk fast. Feeling responsible to the students to cover what I consider a great deal of seriously important content and being caught up in the subject matter, I tend to talk even faster. In the interviews, several students spoke of the difficulty they had keeping up with me during lectures.

Outside of class, I have an open-door policy. I am willing to answer student questions regardless of when they drop by my office, and I conscientiously try to end each conversation with a word or two of encouragement. This availability, however, did not change the students' perceptions of me. During the interviews, many students, particularly the female students, described how they found me unapproachable and standoffish.

The second issue of the study centred on student feedback. If one believes in the value of feedback, then one must take the issue seriously. Feedback from students is one method to evaluate teaching and can lead to real and worthwhile improvements. With the increasing pressures on quality and new emphasis on continuing professional development, listening and responding to the views of students can be helpful.

At times, it takes courage and a willingness to address the identified issues. The purpose of reviewing feedback information is to build on strengths and remedy weaknesses. However, the kind of information collected is a personal choice. So, too, is what one does with the data and the actions subsequently taken.

Gathering data from students is only the beginning. Engaging the students with the findings helps create a climate of trust and respect based on the recognition of teaching and learning as a joint enterprise. I have shared with the students the changes I am making in my presentation style and in the lecture notes so they will see that the comments they have made are being taken seriously. I have noticed an improved atmosphere, a sense of more ease in the classroom.

I am aware that it is not always easy to ask for help. However, engaging in a project with encouraging colleagues interested in discussing various aspects of teaching provides insights into styles and strategies that tend otherwise not to be explicitly articulated. Heads of departments and other senior staff can help develop a culture where it is OK to seek such help as part of one's ongoing professional development. Educational developers are always willing to help and support instructors. New staff are sometimes given mentors who listen, encourage, and offer both practical and personal support. And, it is not just new instructors who can benefit from this kind of input. Staff who have been teaching many years can also profit.

In my case it was important that I had kind and knowledgeable people I could talk to about organizing the project, exploring the results of the study, and planning and implementing the follow up. During this process, I grew as a person and as an instructor.

The third issue addressed by this study was student learning styles. Through the written survey, I was able to identify the learning style preferences of the students in my class. This was important for two reasons. It pointed to a natural block, for some students, in learning to manipulate spatial data, and it brought back into focus my own learning biases. Through this project, I learned that the dominant learning style of the student population during these two semesters was the 'diverger' learning style, as defined by Kolb (1998).

Those who prefer the diverger learning style represent a receptive, experienced-based approach to learning that relies heavily on feeling-based judgements. They prefer to treat each situation as a unique case (Kolb, 1998).

Based on limited observation, I found that acclimatizing to a computer-based course was more difficult for students who preferred concrete experiences. For example, even though the data used for all laboratory sessions in my course refer directly to forested stands, natural water quality, or wildlife habitat and fecundity, many students felt that the digital 'pictures' of the landscape in the computer were not concrete. Moreover, it was difficult for these students to generalize – to take something learned from one example and apply it, in modified form, to another example. Unfortunately, applications of spatial data are not hardwired; the user must be able to evaluate the myriad of options available and select the optimal method of analysis.

With respect to my own learning biases, I am a learner who prefers abstract conceptualization and active experimentation, the direct opposite of the dominant 'concrete' learning style of the students in my class. This makes it more difficult for me to intuit the model-building needs of most of the students in my course. It also makes it difficult for me to identify ahead of time the new hurdles a similar but different example can place before students who learn best through the concrete experience mode.

The fourth issue of this study related to teaching a subject 'at odds' with what students find interesting and enjoyable. It can be a real dilemma for lecturers who are given the task of teaching material which students do not deem worthwhile. This situation can arise for many reasons. It occurs when students have not yet experienced the work world in which the new information or skills are applied, or it can occur when the lecturer does not give adequate attention to supporting student learning on a topic.

In my case, the situation resulted from a relatively new disconnect between the skill set required by the forest industry and resource agencies, and the work preferences of individuals choosing a career in forestry. Five to seven years before I began teaching there began a decline in the need for employees with an 'in the field only' skill set, and, simultaneously, a rapid acceptance of, and, therefore, an increased need for, employees skilled in advanced spatial computing technologies. From the written survey, I learned that students choosing forestry as a profession were doing so primarily because they still believed it was a career that would allow them to work outside in the forests most of the time. The realities of the changing workplace had not yet caught up with the student population.

Student expectations need to be explored at the beginning of a course to highlight such mismatching issues and bring them out into the open. The students studied in this case study wanted their class work to be outdoors as much as possible, and they became frustrated sitting in front of a computer, working in a virtual world instead of the real one. Yet, computers, and spatial data skills in particular, are clearly an important part of their future careers.

The next area that I will address in my teaching is student perceptions of the course content. I will use techniques to increase student knowledge about the usefulness of computers in natural resource management. To start, I will include more natural resource examples of computerized spatial data analyses from current trade journals. I will also start to invite some of my colleagues from my days as an 'in the field' professional to be guest speakers in the classroom. Sometimes it can be very helpful to bring in experts to demonstrate the relevance of certain topics and provide visible evidence of how the skill set is used in practice. In addition, there are times when an external 'expert' can make a point more effectively than an internal 'expert' can. I will ask these forestry professionals to talk about and demonstrate how they use computers and spatial data in their workplace. I will ask them to speak about their personal experiences making management decisions using the data and the many reasons spatial data analyses are a growing part of the work-day world in the forest industry and natural resource management agencies.

Through it all, I will continue to use classroom assessment techniques to monitor:

- the students' grasp of the content;
- the students' feelings about classroom presentations.

REFERENCES

Kolb, D A (1998) Learning styles and disciplinary differences, in *Teaching and Learning in the College Classroom*, ed K A Feldman and M B Paulsen, pp 127–37, Simon & Schuster, Needham Heights, Massachusetts

CHAPTER 11

THIS IS ALL IRRELEVANT!

Case reporters: Peter Knight and Gary Lee

ISSUES RAISED

This case focuses on issues that emerge when one school provides service teaching for another school, especially where there are profound differences over the nature and relevance of what is taught.

BACKGROUND

The case is set in a School of Biomedical Sciences, which is providing service teaching in professional programmes in a Faculty of Health Sciences in an Australian university. The subjects taught include anatomy, physiology, biochemistry, microbiology and pharmacology. None of the Biomedical Sciences teaching staff has qualifications in the professional discipline that is the focus of this case study. Over a period of years, relations between the service school and the students and staff in the commissioning professional school have been deteriorating.

PART 1

'This is all irrelevant!' a student called out in the middle of my lecture on drugs used to control asthma. 'There are many ways of controlling asthma and we should be encouraging people not to use drugs,' she continued. There were shouts of approval from about half of the class and shouts of derision from the other half. What should I do?

I thought that the best I could do was to try to ascertain where the students were getting the idea that medication was bad. I started asking questions, and the answers I received quickly made it apparent that many of the students rejected the 'traditional medical model'. I should not have been surprised. This simply represented a further widening of a long-standing gap between the philosophies of medical science and health care practice. However, it was a concerning development as health professionals holding such a view could endanger patients' lives. It would also tend to isolate them from other health professionals with whom they would be working. I explained that practitioners should not interfere with another clinician's treatment without first consulting him or her. I explained that a non-use of therapeutics in asthma could lead to death in sufferers. I then beat a hasty retreat to try to determine how the scientific basis of health care could ever be promoted to students who were determined to reject the 'medical model'.

I decided the best approach was to consult my Head of School. I was not the only lecturer experiencing problems of this type with this group of students. After some discussion, we decided that our particular problem could be defined as dealing with increasing student antipathy, despite our best efforts to make material relevant to the students' needs.

We decided that we should try to see biomedical sciences through the students' eyes. Of course, the students were training to become part of a profession, so our job was really to discover how the profession saw itself and its role in health care. We believed that part of the problem we were encountering was that many staff in the professional school had themselves rejected the medical model, reflecting the paradigm of practice that was currently driving the profession. By promoting a medical approach, we were putting ourselves at odds with staff as well as students. And the influence of the staff may have had an important role in shaping the students' attitudes to our material.

One obvious theme we could see throughout the profession was the use of models as a way of integrating concepts and providing a basis for practice. The logical conclusion was that it was time to develop a new model that would enable the students to see the biomedical sciences in terms of their framework, and guide lecturers in our school in the presentation of their material. We set about developing our model by consulting textbooks and journals relevant to the profession in question. It was clear that there were certain types of outcomes such as restoration of function and improved functional capacity that were particularly important to this group. Our job then became the identification of where and how biomedical sciences contributed to these outcomes – this would form the basis of our model, and the material we would present.

We decided to emphasize the model approach because it was something the students were interested in, and, more importantly from our point of view, the profession did not expect one model to be accepted to the exclusion of all others. Their emphasis was on the diversity of models, and the different perspectives they provided on a particular problem. We were going to make the most of this.

We thought that the way the material was presented would be important. We could not rely on textbooks or assignments, because all the available material was based on the type of approach we wanted to get avoid. We decided that lectures would be the best way to convey information that was not available anywhere else – to teach biomedical sciences via the back door.

Initially, our own school staff involved in teaching the programme were hesitant (and in some cases hostile) to the idea of creating a new way of presenting biomedical sciences. We were told that changing from the traditional academic model we had used was simply 'conceding defeat', and 'lowering ourselves to uncomfortable standards'. More than once we heard words to the effect that 'nobody from that School is going to tell me how to teach my subject'. It seemed that staff were afraid that their teaching would be corrupted, and that as the experts in the topics, they were the ones best placed to decide what, and especially in this case, how, material was to be taught. We tried to emphasize the fact that the material itself need not change but it was the direction from which the material was being approached that was the issue. Despite our reassurances, lecturers did not greet the new model with open arms.

Nevertheless, we decided to push on. Clearly, we were faced with more than an educational issue. Implementing the new programme would require leadership and change management skills. We decided we would begin by emphasizing the problems we were facing, and the urgency of the changes we proposed. The Head of the School showed his commitment by joining the teaching team and redesigning his lectures to fit the model. We ran a series of seminars for staff, showing that the changes, which were superficially threatening, could be in many ways considered cosmetic. We were looking for a change in style rather than substance. Academic integrity would be maintained. The changes would be in the 'performance aspects' of lecturing. We repeated the message loudly and often.

We agreed that our model needed to be introduced at the beginning of the student's university career, so that it could be accepted as a valid option before strong opinions against the medical model (from which we could not totally remove ourselves) were formed. Consequently, in the first week of their university career, the students received lectures in our courses that were devoted to building an understanding of our model, and how it would apply to their professional careers. Put simply, we told the students what they would be doing when they graduated, and what they would be trying to achieve with their clients (and for many of them, this was really the first time they had thought about it). The profession took a holistic approach to health care, concentrating on the entire individual rather than the functioning of individual systems. Our model was designed to show how various aspects of biomedical science influenced one another and had a role in determining the characteristics of the individual. The interrelationship between the various topics in our subjects and their common contribution to the final product –

a 'functional' human – were the focus of the model. We told the students that their professional goal would be to produce a person who was 'functional', and set about showing how the various aspects of the course – biochemistry, anatomy, neurophysiology, heart and lung function – all contributed to that outcome. Rather than beginning and ending at the basic science, or beginning with the basics and building up, we took the end product and began breaking it down (all the time wondering why it was the medical model that was referred to as reductionist). Throughout the course, new material was introduced by referencing it to our model.

At the end of the first semester of implementation, we anxiously awaited the results of the student surveys. Past years had been very discouraging. At least we knew this year's results could not be any worse – we had not added 'very strongly dislike' to the survey instrument. Initial feedback from the students indicated that they understood and even embraced the model. Yet, they were still somewhat dissatisfied with the material we presented – the surveys told us that students still viewed us as being closely aligned to medicine, even though we had stopped using the classical medical model in our teaching. We wondered what we should do next.

- Why do you think the students were still dissatisfied?
- What would you do next?
- What do you think actually happened next?

PART 2

Our school had always relied heavily on student surveys as a source of feedback on our teaching, so, in order to fine-tune the model, we decided to do an in-depth study of student perceptions. We designed a second questionnaire that we hoped would show us the areas where students were dissatisfied with the course. Although student surveys were a well-established part of the school's culture, we had never before asked questions relating to the actual material presented or the philosophical basis underlying our programmes. Perhaps we had considered these as non-negotiable – another aspect of the lecturer's own sense of subject. We thought that students would welcome the chance to express their views on the material presented. However, eliciting feedback proved difficult, as the students had already been surveyed on a number of issues.

Our survey showed us that students quickly lose patience with excessive attempts to gain their opinions, particularly (as they complained) where there was no clear benefit to them. Despite this reluctance, we pushed on with our examination of their attitudes to our approach. We found that our prelim-inary views were right – students did accept our new model and agreed that it helped them to see the relevance of our material. However, they were suffering from model burnout – they were dissatisfied with the plethora of models they encountered in their professional subjects. Various models of practice were promoted to them by different members of the staff in the professional school. Some of them complained that, although our model was sensible and relevant, our attempts to teach our subjects using a model-based approach, similar to that used by the profession, had simply added another area of potential confusion when it came to defining what the profession was all about. Our subjects had become 'one more model' and students told us that as far as they were concerned they already had more than enough. While student surveys told us that our model had improved student satisfaction, it had opened another area of potential problems.

Another major problem we discovered was the fact that we had failed to embrace the nuances of the profession. Our imperfect attempts to emulate the culture of the profession in our teaching were highlighting the fact that we were not members of that profession. One area where this was obvious was in the language we were using, in particular the word 'patient'. The students saw this as evidence of our medical bias. Their profession made a particular point of emphasizing that they had clients, not patients. By using inappropriate terms, we were inflaming the students' prejudices. Our surveys told us that many students still saw us as wolves in sheep's clothing, trying to appear sympathetic to their profession while still promoting the medical model. Once we stopped referring to patients and began talking about clients, student acceptance, satisfaction and performance in assessments improved dramatically. Mini-surveys at the end of lectures that simply asked students how relevant they found the material showed a dramatic effect. Where we made conscious efforts to use the right language, the surveys showed that students thought the material was much more relevant to them.

The initial resistance of our staff to the changes diminished as the process of implementing the model progressed. Most expressed positive feelings about the experience of redesigning their material. In retrospect, we saw that perhaps we were all in a rut – teaching the same old things in the same old way. Looking at new ways of doing basic things like lecturing had the potential to improve job satisfaction. People also reported that they were enjoying seeing their subject areas from a different perspective. The changed approach even gave people ideas that resulted in new research projects.

Another highlight as far as the staff was concerned was the greater acceptance by the students of the material they were presenting. People had got to the stage where they were reluctant to teach in the programme because of the lack of responsiveness and sometimes outright contempt displayed by the students. After the first semester of implementation, the staff got together and talked about the experience. The consensus was that the students were 'nice people' and 'fun to teach'. Most importantly, they appeared 'genuinely interested' in the lectures. From our experience, it seems clear that relations with the students are an important factor contributing to the satisfaction people get from lecturing.

- What do you think were the major changes that needed to occur before a successful conclusion could be reached?
- Where two different groups are responsible for teaching, how can planning and coordination of approach be achieved?
- What implications for your own teaching can you take from this case?

DISCUSSION

The lack of a direct vocational link between lecturers in our school and the professional courses in which we teach can generate something of a them and us mentality in both students and lecturers. Traditional sciences are viewed by some health science students as belonging to the medical model of health care – a model that is an anathema to them. This view is sometimes endorsed by those teaching the professional subjects in a course. However, our school considered that the basic sciences are important as they provide underpinning knowledge and the links between the various health care professions, enabling them to communicate and work towards the common goal of improving well-being.

In faculties of health sciences, biomedical and behavioural sciences are typically construed as service subjects in health professional courses. Service teaching in these areas provides particular difficulties for lecturers. The very term 'service' teaching denotes that it is different and in some way inferior to 'real' teaching. Tensions can develop between the service school and the professional school. The purchasers of the service teaching often seek to maintain very tight control over the service lecturer's curriculum. Demands for specially tailored or boutique courses may conflict with the efficiencies required to keep the service school functioning.

Service schools react in a number of ways to pressures from professional schools. A traditional way is to insist that the integrity of their discipline be maintained and that students must receive a fundamental understanding of the material. Effectively, this involves resisting demands for boutique courses by focusing on a complete, classical series of lectures. This approach involves a minimum of change on the part of the lecturers. It is the way that they were taught themselves and the way that they know; consequently, it is the comfortable approach for the individual.

This approach seems to offer potential economies of scale, as courses can be delivered to large numbers of students from diverse backgrounds and professional schools. However, providing a generic course to students who have a range of particular needs has the potential to leave students dissatisfied. From the teaching/delivery point of view, it may be a 'cheap' solution but whether it is an optimum use of resources is far more contentious. It may be efficient to say the same words to a large group of students but how effective is it from a student learning point of view?

A second approach is to take the view that service lecturing requires a fundamental commitment to address the desires of the customers. But customers may have only a limited understanding of the material that could be taught. Further, in this case, the service school saw itself as having two customer groups – the professional school itself and their students – and there is no reason why the requirements of the two groups should be the same. In both the service school and the professional school, and in the delivery of health care, knowledge and practice are changing fast. Each group inevitably has a limited understanding of the material and epistemology of the other. A better approach might be to think of the students as the focus of the exercise, as the customers of both professional and service schools. What is in their best interests? This case reinforces the need for more and better communication between learner and teacher, and between teacher and teacher.

In this case, our service school started from the belief that our material provided a common underpinning of knowledge of the basic biomedical sciences that form the basis of the care provided by many of the allied health professions. This common underpinning allows graduates to communicate and function effectively in their multidisciplinary professional environment. In designing our model, our aims were to enable students to develop an understanding of the biomedical sciences, and the medical model that flowed from the basic science. The dangers in this approach were that we would continue to hit professional 'raw nerves' and continue to create animosity towards our material, especially since it was still being designed within our school.

Our curriculum addressed the key issues that we believed should be familiar to health professionals. Our philosophy was that, in training professionals, there is a certain body of knowledge that is essential for successful practice. We could not and would not discard the scientific basis of the material we were teaching, despite the fact that it was not totally accepted by all the staff or students of the school we were servicing. In retrospect, the question arises as to whether the 'non acceptance' of the scientific model was in fact a request for material to be 'more relevant' rather than 'less scientific'.

The challenge in this case is maximizing satisfaction in 'customers' while pursuing an approach to which at least some of them will be fundamentally opposed. There is always a tension between what the students know and do not know and their willingness to tread new ground. It is exactly this tension that we 'service' teachers in this case faced. We increasingly realized that the curriculum, both content and process, was not as 'fixed' as we had previously believed. Our opportunities for improving satisfaction therefore lay with the way in which the material was presented and we focused on this.

In a world where new methods of presenting information seem to be almost de rigueur, the decision to present material by lecturing may appear rather old-fashioned. However, it was a decision taken for several reasons. The first was the absence of appropriate alternate teaching material. As stated above, the course we developed took a new approach to an old subject. No textbooks, CD ROMs or Web pages were available to support our concept. That is not to say they could not have been developed. However, we saw particular advantages in delivering material by lecture – firstly because it allowed us to reinforce the application of the model to the material being presented and the profession which the students are to enter, and second because it allowed us personal contact with the students. The students come from a profession which is very 'people-orientated', and which places great value on personal communications. For this reason, we thought that personal contact would offer the best chance of success. Our view was that good lectures are more than a medium for conveying information. They gave us an opportunity to teach a philosophy at the same time. They also gave us a great deal of flexibility to adjust our material in the short term. We thought that this was particularly important when our teaching was an experiment in progress.

Finally, lecturing was the method that was comfortable to the service teaching staff, which was a good reason for keeping it while effecting change. There are alternatives that would have met the need for immediacy and personal contact – such as problem-based learning (PBL). While the research literature seems to suggest that PBL can be about the same in terms of resource requirements, it would have introduced major issues in terms of changing the 'mindset' of teachers.

The decision to change the philosophical basis underlying the delivery of a course may lead to potential conflicts between the desire of individual lecturers to maintain a personal sense of a subject and the group goal of achieving specific learning outcomes with students. The greater the amount of talking, planning, monitoring and evaluating among and between people, the better the chance of agreeing and effecting the learning outcomes. Implementing such a process is a crucial role for management.

In assessing the effectiveness of our changes, we were conscious of the need to use objective measures. Service teaching has two customers: students in classes and commissioning departments. The question arises as to which of the customers should be assessing outcomes, and whose needs are paramount. An important decision to be made in the planning of service teaching is whether it is better to be 'all things to all people', or to focus all efforts on improving outcomes in a particular customer group. In this case, the view was taken that student outcomes should take precedence. However, optimizing outcomes for students may not result in optimal outcomes in the eyes of the professional school. Our decision to place greater weight on the student's opinions was rationalized on the basis that it is very likely that the school would be guided by the feedback from its students – that their reports would be important in forming the school's view of our services.

Those implementing particular teaching models may find themselves addressing issues of leadership, change management and potentially, industrial relations. As assessments and reporting of educational quality become more commonplace and student satisfaction assumes a more prominent position in the assessment of educational quality, such issues will arise more frequently. The challenge in lecturing is improving student understanding and increasing student satisfaction. In our experience, improvements in student satisfaction were accompanied by improvements in lecturers' satisfaction. The teaching environment became less adversarial and there appeared to be real gratitude on the part of the students for the efforts we had made to meet their needs. And this perhaps is the key point of our case. We confronted the issues posed by student feedback, we left our comfort zones, we made changes, these were not immediately successful, we then made more changes, and everyone was happier with the result.

As we look back on our experience there are several lessons that become apparent. The first is that it is possible to make changes in lecturing content, to conceive of material in a different way. Such changes can increase student satisfaction and may increase lecturer satisfaction. We found that the use of a model with clearly defined outcomes helped us to deliver a coordinated course, and remove some of the variability in individual staff responses that can affect quality. The content was conceived by the teachers, not as an idiosyncratic 'right' but as a coordinated 'whole' and this made more sense to the students. We created what we thought was the best possible product and then showed people why they should use it. Finally, through changing the conceptual frame by introducing a model-based approach for delivery of content we got an entirely different reaction from the audience. This is a significant issue, not just in lecturing but also in the entire sphere of education, where so many new methods of delivering material are being tried. Ultimately, by connecting with the students and other staff, good outcomes can be achieved. The key to success in this case study was finding a way to make the connection.

PERSONAL REFLECTION

- What is the link between student satisfaction and the quality of student learning? Can a dissatisfied student connect with a course?
- How do you implement a team approach with colleagues in planning, monitoring and evaluating courses on which you teach?
- What or who drives change in your organization? Would your response to demands for change differ according to who was driving the change?
- What are the privileged and underprivileged teaching tasks in your department? Why? How could teaching be improved in the 'underprivileged' courses?

CHAPTER 12

Getting sacked

Case reporter: Phil Race

ISSUES RAISED

This case raises the issues of a visiting lecturer being inadequately briefed and ending up with very hostile but not necessarily representative feedback from a small group of students.

BACKGROUND

The case occurred at a large metropolitan university in the UK. A male lecturer from another institution is invited to run a guest session on 'Assessment and Learning' with a group of university teachers undertaking a continuing professional development programme, some of whom turned out to be very experienced.

PART 1

I did not expect any trouble. I had often done this sort of thing before. In fact, I felt like an 'expert witness' on learning and assessment and normally had a good time when I did a slot at other universities on this, my favourite topic. As someone who often does guest appearances, I did not feel nervous at the prospect of meeting 50 or so new faces, and taking the class through the key points of my thinking on one of my most passionate interests. My lecture was to be the second input on the first day of a three-day short course.

I had done my homework. I had sent copies of my paper on assessment and learning in advance and checked that it would be reproduced for all the class members. I had prepared my PowerPoint presentation, and even had back-up overheads with me, in case the data projector did not turn up. I set off on a train two hours earlier than the one that would have got me to my destination just in time and duly arrived at the campus in plenty of time for my session which started at 11 o'clock.

I could not get into the room until half past ten, as the class had another session up to then, followed by a coffee break. I noticed that the room was over-full. Most of the students were seated at upright chairs with swivel arm tables for note taking, but at the back of the room were several low armchairs without tables, and these too were occupied.

My understanding was that all of the students were roughly in the same position and had not had any particular previous experience of training about assessment and learning, so I could work with the group as a homogeneous whole. I intended to guide them along my pre-planned sequence that included inputs from me and short individual and group exercises for them. I introduced myself and set out along the by now familiar path of challenging the preconceptions of the class about assessment and learning, and then introducing the ideas I hoped they would find really interesting and useful. I knew right away that it was not going to be my best-ever session: I had a catchy throat and a cold was coming on. At one point, I just about lost my voice, but no problem, with all my experience of giving students things to do, I had a short task for the group until I found a throat pastille and regained my voice.

Two of the normal course lecturers were among the audience, and I had chatted briefly to them before starting, and used them as a barometer at various points in my presentation, bringing them in when I wanted reactions to key issues. They seemed perfectly happy throughout the session and nodded their agreement to one or two of my more provocative thoughts about assessment practice. The Course Director herself could not be at my session and had sent her apologies.

I could tell two things about the 50 students. Those close to me (on the upright chairs) were hanging on my every word and were obviously interested. But at the back of the room, in the low armchairs, I could just make out that the dimly lit faces were impassive. From that part of the room, there were no smiles when I included anecdotes to capture or recapture interest.

About halfway through came a challenging question – from the back of course. It was from one of the passive armchair students. She was quite rude, really, and posed her question when I was halfway through one of my key points. It was not a question that was relevant at that point. In fact, the question showed that she was already diametrically opposed to one of the ideas I was going to suggest a little later. I replied, 'Yes indeed, we'll be looking right at that issue in just five minutes or so', and carried on. She looked none-too-pleased but I pressed on. The difference between the bright-eyed students at the front and those in the armchairs continued and I was aware that there were mutterings and whisperings coming from the back. 'Not very professional of them,' I mused to myself as I pressed on.

At the end of the session, it was lunch break for the group, and going home time for me. Two or three of the students who had been at the front came up to me and said what a good session it had been, and agreed with one or other of the criticisms I had been airing about the overuse of traditional assessment formats (particularly unseen written time-constrained examinations). OK, I thought. It had not been my most stunning performance and I had not carried the whole group, but I had won the day with at least some of the students.

What happened next therefore was a surprise. It was an unpleasant surprise! Feedback from the class had been collected at the end of the short course and the feedback about my session was critical. A message from the Course Director was left on my answering machine at home telling me this and cancelling a similar input that had been arranged for three months' time with another group.

- Why do you think the armchair students behaved as they did?
- How do you think the presenter dealt with the classroom situation as it developed?
- Could anything have been done differently?
- What would you do next?
- What do you think happened next?

PART 2

I could not believe it. After all, students had come up to me at the end of the session and chatted very amicably with me about it. But I take feedback seriously and rang back to ask for more detail. It was agreed that photocopies of the main criticisms would be posted to me. I waited uncomfortably for some days for these to arrive, and arrive they did. It turned out that three students had written really quite damning reports about my lecture, accusing me of arrogance, hostility (yes, that was included in the words on their comments) and various other crimes. It was quite clear to me that the three students had talked together about my session, as the wording of their comments, and even the order of their complaints, was far too similar to have been a matter of chance. Apparently most of the other students had not completed any handwritten comments relating to my particular session on their feedback forms, so there was just the critical feedback from the three students to go on.

I was quite devastated. I had not received this sort of vitriolic feedback before. On reflection, I thought that I might have been a bit 'bullish' on the day, trying to sweep the whole group forward on my train of thought and believing that I had most of them with me. But did I deserve this? I rang up one of the lecturers who had been there to see what she thought. She seemed as shocked as I was at the hostile feedback. She had enjoyed the session herself and had heard positive comments from some of the other students. However, the ensuing conversation revealed two things I had not known.

Firstly, the whole cohort was required to be at this three-day course; their attendance had been made mandatory. Secondly, some were not (as I had supposed) new to assessment and learning; indeed, some had a lot of experience of both and were experienced practitioners. I had thought that they were all new to assessment! The cohort had included at least a few students who believed (quite rightly) that their experience should have been taken into account, that they should not have been required to be at this introductory short course at all, or should have at least been allowed to drop in and out of it as they pleased.

It now began to make sense to me and I rationalized the situation as follows:

- the evidence was actually that only three of 50 students had been really critical of my session;
- I did not know that these people were required to be there and were resentful about this in the first place;
- the Course Director had not been able to attend herself, so had reacted to the feedback that she was given, without knowing that most of the students may not have felt anything like so strongly about my session as the three whose feedback she was given.

However, such rationalizations did not comfort me much. It did not comfort me at all in fact. After all, I had been sacked! I had had a future lecture cancelled summarily. I had never been sacked before. I have never been sacked since.

Was it just that I had had a bad day? I had been at the start of a cold after all. In fact, the cold ran its course quite heavily during the next weekend, the way they do. But no, I had not thought I was having a bad day, I had thought I was doing well enough. 'What should I have done differently?' I kept asking myself. I was hurt and I was angry with the Course Director. Surely, she should have briefed me more carefully. It turned out that she had been off ill herself. Even so, I thought that she should not have reacted so strongly to what turned out to be only three disgruntled students.

My confidence had had a serious knock. What was I to do in the future as I met new groups at different institutions, having been invited to give my guest input on assessment and learning to yet more groups of professional mature part-time students? And what about my published paper on assessment? Was the paper a bad one too? Should I stop trying to challenge student preconceptions about assessment and learning and stick to other things that I knew I did well? Or should I just shrug off the incident and not overreact. Whatever I choose, this had had an enormous effect on me.

- What advice would you offer at this point?
- Have you had a similar experience that has affected your confidence? How did you react?

DISCUSSION

It took a long time for me to get over this incident. Actually, I do not think I shall ever quite get over it, but now I hope that I am equipped with some tactics to protect me from the events that I have described.

Three years on from that fateful Monday, I now do things a little differently:

- I try to find out more about the people in each new group. I ask whether they are experienced in what I am going to talk about. I use 'show of hands' techniques to measure their agreement or disagreement about ideas. 'How many of you have already done so-and-so?' I ask quite often.
- I try not to keep to my pre-prepared sequence when there are signals to tell me that it is not appropriate for the group I am with. I still use PowerPoint, but I have an action button hidden at the bottom right-hand corner of each slide. That action button takes me, at a click of the mouse, to a 'Choices' slide, with twenty-odd short slide sequences from which to choose. I can now skip those parts of any presentation that are preaching to the converted or that are simply of no interest to my audience. I can now move on to address, straight away, an important question from a member of the audience, and often do. I can 'escape' from any of my diversions and get back either to my 'Choices' slide, or back to the original point in my presentation (should this be where I really want to go – although usually the reason for diverting is that it is not!).
- I take more notice of the faces at the back of the room. Where possible, I make sure that there are not any comfortable armchairs lurking there! I try to involve people at the back, rather than pay too much attention to those who look interested at the front.

I have not (so far) been sacked again! However, I am continuously aware that I could so easily slip back into the sequence of errors that characterized that fateful Monday. And I continue to look for further ways of making sure that I never get myself into the same position again.

PART 4

AUTHENTICITY: LIVING YOUR VALUES IN LECTURES

CHAPTER 13

LEARNING FROM THE INSIDE OUT

Case reporter: Peter Frederick

ISSUES RAISED

This case raises the issue of starting from students' own lives and experiences in order to encourage a deep approach to learning.

BACKGROUND

The case occurred at a US liberal arts college. An experienced male lecturer with a national reputation as an educational innovator and a local one as a pedagogical and political 'Berkeley' radical was asked to lecture to 30, 18–22-year-old students on American Indian History and Cultures.

PART 1

In truth, I had mellowed a bit since my early career at Berkeley in the 1960s. For example, despite student urgings, I had steadfastly resisted pressure to teach a course on the American Indians because I sensed that student motivations were based on romantic notions of a mythical Indian rather than on the rigorous quest for historical and cultural truths. I also feared the same instinct to romanticize Indians in myself.

Events intervened to change my mind. On the basis of an article I had written on how to lead discussions, in the late 1980s I was invited twice to Sinte Gleska, an Indian tribal college on the Rosebud reservation in South Dakota. The purpose of the first visit was to take a workshop with the staff on discussions as they had been having difficulty getting their students to participate in discussions. As a result of some research on Indian education and Lakota culture, my hunch, which turned out to be right, was that the faculty, half white and half native yet all educated in Euro-American universities, were using a Socratic model of discussion. Indian culture discouraged expressive individualism; that is, individual students were socialized not to raise their hands and engage in the kind of one-on-one interchange with a professor that defined the Socratic approach. So they remained silent. My focus on a collaborative, small group model of discussion came as an obvious remedy.

The second visit, a year later, was intended to observe classes, witness the changes in faculty and student behaviour, and make further suggestions for interactive strategies. I took away far more learning from Sinte Gleska, however, than I brought. I acquired many teaching materials and ideas, to be sure, but the most significant and lasting result of my visit was the commitment finally to lecture on an Indian history course.

I was excited about teaching the course, especially the determination to resist the temptation to give a formal lecture presentation and instead to add to my repertoire of innovative pedagogical strategies. The course began with a highly challenging, theoretical book on the nature of the primarily Plains Indian religious and philosophical world view, as expressed in Indian art and other artefacts. The work, *The Primal Mind: Vision and reality in Indian America* by Jamake Highwater, soon to be a discredited person for his dubious claims of Indian ancestry, was obtuse and difficult. Yet it was brilliant in its contrasts of Indian and Anglo-American views of nature, land and landscapes, forms of religious and artistic expression, family and social relationships, and the sacred.

There was a certain amount of tension on the day we began our discussion of the first two sections of Highwater's book. In the past I would have given a summary lecture on Highwater's ideas to provide a foundation for the students' understanding of the text. But now my goal for this first encounter was for students to discover his ideas for themselves, and thereby own the learning. I was not sure it would work. As I entered the classroom, I sensed the students' uneasiness and insecurity about their ability to explain the book, yet I was determined not to resort to a didactic lecture when faced with student silence. Instead, I relied on a usually effective way into a discussion by asking the students at the beginning of class to take a few moments to write a paragraph stating what they thought were some of Highwater's major ideas. After five minutes or so, I then invited them to pair off and talk to one another about their paragraphs. All this was tried and true, good pedagogy for launching into a discussion of difficult material (think, pair, share, discuss).

I noticed their unease as they spoke with one another, and the awkward silence of some of the pairs. Undaunted, after a few moments I asked to hear some examples of their writing. Reluctantly, and only after great prodding, several students read their paragraphs. They were terrible! Although it was clear they had read the essay, their statements missed the message. I felt crushed, discouraged, even a bit angry. Had they done the reading? Had they read carefully enough? Clearly, they had failed to capture the gist of what Highwater was saying. I acknowledged that I understood this was a difficult reading, but we were not getting where we needed to be.

At this point I asked an especially good student, whom I knew from a previous course, to read his paragraph. Surely this would move us along. But even he failed to summarize the essence of the reading, and I felt further discouraged. 'Good effort, William,' I said with a bit of false bravado, 'but we still are not getting it.' Pause. 'Then why don't you tell us,' he said; it was more of a demand than a question. The room got very, very silent. I worried that I had given them too hard a task, that they were unable to discover difficult culturally new concepts for themselves. I could feel my heart pounding as the class waited for my response to William's challenging question. Should I tell them?

- What should the teacher do?
- What would you do in this situation?

PART 2

From where inside me I cannot say (my experiences at Sinte Gleska?, my own inspiration drawn from Highwater?), I instinctively said, 'Draw a picture of it.'

'Huh?!' several students responded, all with quizzical looks on their faces.

'Draw a picture of it,' I repeated. 'Draw a picture of Highwater's ideas, his message.'

Some students repeated their 'Huh?!' but several others went immediately to work, clearly energized. Still others stared into space, or glanced nervously at their colleagues who were busily drawing. One by one, however, every student set to work drawing a picture, some with clearly excited ideational light bulbs going off in their heads, others more cautiously, struggling to put something down tentatively into a drawing. I was aware of the room bursting with creative energy.

Ecstatic with the mood, I worked the room, peering over shoulders to see how they were doing, affirming their work and creativity, offering encouragement, acknowledging that being a 'good artist' was not important, asking an occasional question. In a rather short time, most were finished. Many of the drawings were brilliantly imaginative, clever visual representations of philosophical ideas. They were expressed in abstract images, capturing a holistic sense of an integrated culture, contrasted with the more fragmented Western culture. Some students resorted to stick figures, Indians and whites, circles and squares, in struggle and conflict, or with two clearly delineated sections to the drawing. That was OK, too. They seemed, after all, to understand Highwater's ideas.

Again, on an instinct, for I had not planned this, I invited the students to stand up and move around the room, looking at one another's drawings, asking questions of one another. 'What were you trying to do?', 'What does that represent?', 'Why did you put that there?' Sometimes, I heard comments such as, 'Oh, of course, now I see! I get it now!' The cumulative affect of looking at several different ways of expressing Highwater's ideas deepened their evolving understanding. To hasten the process and provide some closure, I invited a few students to go to the board and explain their drawing to the whole class. I remember an Art major, normally quiet in discussions, having his moment of stardom as he explained his highly symbolic design to the class, and glowing! The whole process was, in fact, one of several mini-lectures on the book, not by me but by many different students. I was thrilled! We were not only explaining Highwater's difficult ideas but also modelling a redefinition of 'lecture' – and lecturers!

Encouraged by the success of this experience, I continued to experiment with visual representations of knowledge in this and other courses. But by innovating in these ways I worried that I was straying too far from my training in rigorous scholarship and that we were romanticizing the American Indians.

Four years later I am teaching the same course, though much revised. I am now using several different books and focussing more and more on the Plains Indians (Crow, Cheyenne, Lakota Sioux). Two quotations on the first page of the syllabus are intended to state this essential tension in the goals of the course, and to give the students a problem of dissonance immediately. The first, by Michael Dorris, reads:

> We can stop treating Indians like sacred, one-dimensional European myths and begin the hard, terribly difficult and unpredictable quest of regarding them as human beings.

The second, by Henrietta Whiteman (whose Indian, Cheyenne name is White Buffalo Woman), says:

> Cheyenne history, and by extension Indian history, in all probability will never be incorporated into American history, because it is holistic, human, personal, and sacred.

What?!? Who are these people we will be studying: unique reflections of particular cultures, or universally human? Inherently imbued with the sacred, or falsely one-dimensionally sacred? An autobiographical exercise with the students, in which they represent their life themes visually in pictographic form (a Plains Indian art form), reveals to students the unique and universal aspects of their own development.

We are several weeks into the course and I am still worrying about the tension. The students respond to the visuals but I wonder if they understand the texts rigorously. Our next book, by Peter Nabokov, is on a minor Crow figure; it is titled *Two-Leggings: The making of a crow warrior*, published in 1967. Two-Leggings was a rather insignificant pipe-holder, never having reached the status of a chief. The book, based on the ethnographic interviews of William Wildschut with Two-Leggings between 1919 and his death in 1923, is essentially a coming-of-age story. It is, though, a challenging book, like Highwater, but for different reasons.

Without chronology or context, other than Nabokov's chapter arrange-ments of the disconnected stories recorded by Wildschut, Two-Leggings tells dozens of stories about a plethora of incidents in his life, most during his early manhood – his teenage years and early 20s. The book is filled with 'coup stories', heroic tales of the valorous deeds of a young Crow male; they are concrete, detailed and almost entirely without reflection or causal connection.

Two-Leggings's stories include: seeking acceptance from his older brothers and tribal medicine men; hunting his first buffalo and looking for food; trying to gain 'good medicine' for protection; raiding parties against enemy Indian nations; getting a wife; and gaining respect as a leader. The quest for acceptance and recognition, usually denied because of his many flawed actions, consumed his attentions. This theme, however, was difficult to detect buried in the many stories of Two-Leggings's error-filled raids, embarrassing tests of manhood, and failed vision quests.

I had read the book carefully, taught it before and mastered the content, themes and unique structure. I was tempted to explain all this to the students, but resisted in order for them to discover the rich ethnographic and historical material for themselves. But Two-Leggings was a difficult book to read, remember and discuss. Without linearity or structure (other than Nabokov's chapters) the numerous incidents of Two-Leggings's life all ran together, were mostly unreflective, and without connection.

I was not sure how to discuss the book, so I approached the class for our first discussion of the book with some concerns. My problem was how best to start? How to make the text accessible for the students? How to open up the themes in Two-Leggings's life and in young male Crow culture? How to help them understand both what was unique to Crow warrior culture and what was universal to the human experience? As I entered the room, a bit nervously, Sean's comment was hardly reassuring: 'I thought I would like this,' he said, 'but it was hard! I found it rough going.' Others echoed his complaint. Again, there was silence waiting for my response. What should I do?

- What would you do? How would you start the discussion of Two-Leggings?
- What strategies (other than visualizations) do you think the lecturer used?

PART 3

This time I had a plan. Without even mentioning Two-Leggings, I invited the students to recall their teenage years and to tell a story of a moment when they sought or achieved a great personal triumph and recognition. 'Do not be shy,' I told them, 'tell a story about a moment in your life when you were the hero.' No problems here; they went right to it. They wrote, they spoke in pairs, and then I invited testimonies, examples of their heroic moments. We listened for themes and patterns. Out came their emotional stories of football games, swimming and other sports triumphs, musical achievements and, for many, notable failures. Despite the instructions, several students chose stories of failure (as Two-Leggings did) rather than heroic victories. We heard stories not only about winning goals, home runs, best times, public-speaking awards, high marks on examinations, but also about missed goals, 'pulling my little brother out of the swimming pool', a first drunken spree, 'the time I had to call my father from jail to come bail me out', surviving a canoe spill on a raging river, and many others.

I was thrilled with the intensity of their experiences and the way the mood of the class, initially somewhat hostile, had changed. In debriefing the themes and patterns of their stories, the transition to Two-Leggings's life and themes was natural and easy. Students listed similarities and differences, noted aspects unique to Crow culture, to their own, and universal human qualities. They understood that, in a way, they were telling their own versions of 'coup stories'. We explored the extent to which the stories were uniquely male, thus raising gender issues. We explored issues of stages of psychological development and the extent to which young people are defined and constrained by cultural characteristics. We struggled with the phenomenon of Two-Leggings's intense aspirations for recognition and respect with his all-too-frequent self-induced huge failures and embarrassments. Through the medium of stories, albeit indirect ones, we did, in fact, analyse Nabokov's book with considerable depth.

But we were not finished. There was much more in the book we had not dealt with. For example, although we had explored many of the themes in Two-Leggings's life we had not discussed the form of his telling: concrete, literal, non-linear and unreflective. Therefore, on the second day of class, with warning, I gave the students a test over the book and its detailed content. It was a very difficult test: concrete, literal, non-linear and unreflective. Although they worked in small groups, the test was shamelessly at a lower level of recollection and memory. The students suffered but plugged away at it, doing the best they could but letting me know how picky and unfair they thought the questions were. Feigning concern, I actually was delighting in their misery, much of which I suspected was also feigned.

I graded the test with them during the lecture (as hunting and raiding behaviour were 'graded' by Crow elders), and they kept an account of how well they were doing (as Two-Leggings constantly did). They did not do very well, and agonized over how seriously I – the elder – was going to take their marks (as Two-Leggings did). I had rarely given an examination that evoked as many emotional responses as this one. Written essays are thinking exercises in which students apply reason to a problem; this one tested memory and elicited (understandable) howls of outrage and unfairness.

In debriefing the 'test', which I had given obviously more for heuristic purposes than accounting ones, we in fact deepened our exploration of the content and analysis of Nabokov's book, and of Crow warrior culture. The students experienced again the concrete, non-linear nature of young male Crow thinking and reporting. Although they were relatively sure I was not going to count their marks, they nevertheless sought to get every detailed answer down right, especially as we went over the test. They argued vociferously over details such as names and places to gain a point (as Two-Leggings did). In going over the test, including its form and format as well as the right answers, we shed further understanding on Crow warrior culture. In fact, we never precisely and systematically discussed Nabokov's book, except indirectly by debriefing first their stories and second the test.

- It could be argued that this approach is only appropriate for 'humanities' subjects. Do you agree?
- Could this kind of approach be used in a much larger class? Would any changes need to be made?
- Can you think of ways in which you could use the lives and experiences of your own students to encourage learning?

DISCUSSION

We now understand that learning is a dual process in which, initially, the inside beliefs and understandings must come out, and only then can something outside get in... To prompt learning, you've got to begin with the process of going from inside out. The first influence on new learning is not what teachers do pedagogically but the learning that's already inside the learner.
(Shulman, 1999)

'Stories,' Joan Didion has written, 'fill in the space between what happened and what it means.' In our discussion of Two-Leggings, we moved from student stories to Crow cultural meaning, from their 'inside' to the content 'outside', in Lee Shulman's terms. Shulman's focus on learning from 'the inside out' is central to understanding the pedagogies described in this case.

At the critical juncture in both parts of the story, I delayed bringing in ideas from outside the two difficult texts until I had brought out what was already inside the students' own experience and awareness. By honouring the students' internalized visual representations of their experience with a book and their own familiar coming-of-age stories, I was able, perhaps ironically, to help students access the culturally different and unfamiliar aspects of native American experience and thought. Through visualizations and stories, the students began from inside themselves in order to connect with and learn ideas from the outside. Starting from what they knew helped to give them confidence. I was also able to move away from the traditional notion of a lecture and have the courage to try a whole range of different techniques. Some of these techniques came from prior experiences, others I tried on the spot. So often we have a plan or formula of what we wish to achieve only to experience or 'sense' the plan does not always work. What I was doing was reflecting on my past experience, putting the 'reflective practitioner' to work in the classroom and making a conscious decision to change directions. That sometimes takes courage and a willingness to change activities on the spot. But the consequences of not making those reflective 'intuitive' changes may be detrimental to student learning. Lecturing is not simply a formulaic exercise of following a set of rules but rather something that can be developed and enhanced through experience and learning from others.

Pedagogical strategies that help students understand diverse, unfamiliar cultures are also effective for all kinds of subjects. Deep learning is more likely to occur when students are able to connect their lives, passions and prior experiences with crucial core course concepts. Recall Shulman writing that, for learning, 'the inside beliefs and understandings must come out, and only then can something outside get in'. In other words, students must be given opportunities to construct their own understanding of new knowledge, to form their own pedagogical representations of difficult concepts based on what they already know inside.

These observations are consistent with the 'deep learning' principles of current learning theory, represented by Paul Ramsden in Australia and Lee Shulman in the United States. In a useful summary on *What We Know About Learning*, reflecting much of the work at the Oxford Brooks Centre for Staff Development, Ewell (1997) suggests, among other principles, that 'direct experience decisively shapes individual understanding' and that learning is about each individual 'making meaning... by establishing and reworking patterns, relationships, and connections'. He also writes, consistent with Shulman's work, that learning happens best actively and in interaction with others, 'in a cultural context that provides both enjoyable interaction and substantial personal support'.

Rather intense emotions were present in the visualizations, stories and 'test' described in this case. I am intrigued by the growing body of literature on the role of emotions in learning and its inextricable connection with the intellect; that is, the synergistic interplay of affect and cognition for deep learning. Recently, Robert S Root-Bernstein, a physiologist at Michigan State, and Michele Root-Bernstein, a writer and historian, have pointed out the many ways in which learning is enhanced by an emotional dimension. They cite, as one among many examples, the work of botanist Barbara McClintock as she develops 'a feeling for the organism' in order to understand and describe an ear of corn. 'Creative thinking,' the Root-Bernsteins write, 'relies on what the philosopher Michael Polanyi has called "personal knowledge": images, patterns, sensual and muscular feelings, play-acting, empathising, emotions, and intuitions' (Root-Bernstein and Root-Bernstein, 2000). In this case it was precisely in the formation of these visual images, in the empathic affect of shared stories, and in play-acting a test, that students connected their lives with – and therefore better understood – the culturally different (and humanly similar) lives of native Americans.

Current popular work on 'emotional intelligence' is another aspect of the connection between affect and cognition. But the basis is deeper than that. In a fascinating book by Antonio Damasio, *Descartes' Error: Emotion, reason, and the human brain* (1994), the author argues that 'emotions and feelings may not be intruders in the bastion of reason' but rather are 'enmeshed in its networks, for worse and for better'. Damasio, along with other cognitive psychologists, explains the physiological connections between the amygdala (locus of emotions) and limbic system of the brain with the outer cortex and other areas of reason. One function of the cortex is to map and integrate signals from the body, including emotional reactions. Therefore, reasoned emotional experiences enhance critical thinking; mind, body and feelings are all involved in a holistic process of learning. And spirit, too?

Appropriately, native peoples themselves have long understood these principles of deep learning. While at Sinte Gleska I was shown a book, *The Sacred Tree*, used in first-year English writing courses that featured the sacred symbol of the medicine wheel. In a twice-bisected circle are four quadrants representing, variously for Plains cultures, the four directions, the four winds, the four cardinal virtues of the Lakota people and the four sacred principles of the Cheyenne. There are two polarities in the representational drawing of the medicine wheel in *The Sacred Tree*: the mental and emotional (North and South) and the physical and spiritual (West and East). These also, of course, represent Carl Jung's fourfold function of the mind: thinking and feeling, sensation and intuition. Taken together, these four aspects form the basis for holistic learning, strongly reflecting the integral relationship between affect and cognition. Perhaps I have not entirely overcome the temptation to romanticize the Indians after all.

REFERENCES

Damasio, A (1994) De*scartes' Error: Emotion, reason, and the human brain*, C P Putnam's Sons, New York

Didion, J (1978) Telling stories, The Friends of Bancroft Library, University of California, Berkeley

Ewell, P (1997) What we know about learning, *American Association of Higher Education Bulletin*, **50**, pp 3–6

Root-Bernstein, R S and Root-Bernstein, M (2000) Learning to think with emotion, *The Chronicle of Higher Education*, January 14, p 64

Shulman, L (1999) Taking learning seriously, *Change*, **31** (4), pp 11–17

Whiteman, H (1987) White buffalo woman, in *The American Indian and the Problem of History*, ed C Martin, Oxford University Press, New York

CHAPTER 14

TEACHING POWER

Case reporter: Lyn Carson

ISSUES RAISED

This case focuses on issues that arise when a lecturer has to decide whether to use participatory teaching methods that have been successful with small classes, in a large group, traditional lecture theatre setting. It also raises the issue of consistency between the teacher's theory and practice, as participatory democracy and power are both the subject of the course and an issue in the way that it is taught.

BACKGROUND

This case took place at the University of Sydney: a large, metropolitan, research-based university with large classes. The students ranged in age from school leavers to mature-aged students. The teacher had formerly used participatory methods successfully with classes at a small regional university.

PART 1

Before moving to the city, I had taught small classes (up to 25 students) with most students studying at a distance. I saw myself as innovative and idealistic. My courses in a regional university were student based and students had considerable control over the content and the teaching strategies. For example, I made detailed comments on ungraded assignments that were set quite early in the semester and I introduced pre-semester questionnaires to gauge student entry levels and repeated these during the semester to check the progress of students.

I adopted and then refined a method that allowed me to extract weekly feedback from students. The method of instant feedback was similar to the one-minute paper that is used by teachers to take the pulse of a class. I wanted to add an extra dimension – reciprocity – a key component of democratic practice. This was accomplished by feeding back to students a summary of their comments and supplementing this with my own reflections on their learning and the group experience.

I offered students pieces of paper at the end of every session. Previously prepared sheets with typed questions proved ineffective because unanticipated questions often arose during the teaching period. Instead, a 'prompt' question was written on the board and students were asked to reply anonymously. They left their comments at the door as they left. They expected that their responses would be fed back to them at the start of the next session. I typed the comments into my computer because I noticed that this recording was quite an important aspect of my own learning. I was more likely to heed the words and to reflect on them if I physically typed them. It slowed down the speed of my thinking and made me more attuned to new or subtle information.

Receiving feedback from students was the first part of this process. Engaging with students about their feedback and sometimes altering the course content or the teaching strategies were the necessary responses that followed. In starting each session with feedback from the previous one, some discussion inevitably occurred and this occasionally meant fireworks! A break-out in democracy is never dull. A controversial issue might be raised and I needed to be flexible enough to respond to this with the entire group's input. It might lead to some lively debate, or fiery challenges, particularly as the group's confidence increased. They would become bolder as the semester unfolded and as they began to realize that genuine listening was occurring and their concerns and suggestions were being acted upon.

I was teaching Australian politics and was a former elected representative with a fascination for democratic principles, the area of my applied research. So during five years of teaching before going to Sydney, my efforts had become increasingly focused on power sharing in the classroom. I had sought to give students greater control over their learning environment and to develop teaching strategies that could be adapted immediately to meet students' needs. My teaching practice was beginning to resemble my democratic ideals. It all seemed to be working well, but then...

I took up a position with the University of Sydney, a major metropolitan university. I taught a unit in political sociology – power in society. When I encountered my first class of 200 students I wondered how my democratic ideals and my deep desire to share power was going to find expression amongst this mob. It was ever thus. It has been the dilemma of democrats for eons – matching practice with ideals. Having told the group about my democratic intentions, I was left with the unenviable task of proving congruence between my espoused theory and my theory-in-use.

With smaller groups, this had become relatively straightforward; their feedback had been able to alter the course content or the teaching strategies. For example, in one political theory class at the regional university, students said they wanted more lectures because they found the class overly democratic. They wanted more input. I responded by giving them 15-minute talks with overhead transparencies, just as they had requested. In addition, I contributed my own feedback about the nature of the course that was based on discovery learning. A compromise was reached and the lecture time was used to summarize students' own work, rather than give them the 'answers'. Any unresolved problems or questions were drawn out. Their later feedback showed that this was helping them to consolidate their own discoveries and it enabled me to uncover gaps in their knowledge base. Changing direction and experimenting with new approaches had been very easy with a class of 20. Looking at this lecture hall of 200 students, changing direction seemed a bit like attempting to turn an ocean liner.

Interestingly one of my lectures addressed the problem of achieving democratic outcomes as populations grow. Intuitively we consider that democracy is more likely to occur in a small group than it is in a large one. Participatory democracy in my experience had been more achievable in local government, for example, than at national level. However, a contrary view exists and that is that enabling democratic outcomes in small groups is just as difficult to achieve as it is in nation states. The best we can hope for are circumstances where a breakout of democracy can occur. This position states also that the best groundwork we can do is to create an environment in which this is more likely to take place. A similar problem confronted me as I faced this large class – how was I to replicate my successful feedback/response loop when working with hundreds of students?

My inner turmoil grew and a number of questions began to dominate my thoughts: how would I create an environment in which democracy could break out and what extra difficulties arise in a large lecture format using a reciprocal feedback system? After the first lecture, I was left with hundreds of scraps of paper and the logistical impossibility of typing up 200 responses from future sessions. The best I could do was to read them all hurriedly, then summarize the major points. How could I respond to suggestions? I was bound by a timetable and descriptions of lectures that were distributed at the start of semester. I could hear the students concerns but would be unable to respond with any meaningful changes. What would democracy look like if it broke out in a lecture hall? I realized I was as fearful of the mob as those who had questioned the ideals of Thomas Jefferson had been. How was it possible to teach experientially given the physical constraints of a lecture hall? So many unanswerable questions confronted me and it seemed as though I was collapsing under the weight of the power that I did not want or need, but I could not fathom how to give it away.

- What do you think the lecturer actually did?
- What would you have done in this situation?
- What experiential strategies do you think could be used given the physical constraints of a large group and tiered lecture hall?

PART 2

The unit of study, the cumbersome ocean liner, changed its direction as only ocean liners can – very slowly and very painstakingly. There are none so determined as political activists. In my younger days I had chained myself to factory farms, withstood pressure hoses directed at me as I straddled the deck of a live-sheep carrier, faced abusive punters at a steeplechase. I was used to defending the voiceless and here was another opportunity. I decided that I could handle a few hundred friendly students who seemed as perplexed as I did about how to find their voice in such an incongruous setting.

Firstly, I tackled the challenge posed by my 'flexible' questions. I wrote the question on the board at the beginning of the session for students to notice and think about throughout the lecture. This meant that the method of feedback was more closely aligned with the teaching of a specific concept – the question might be, for example, 'What do you understood by the term deliberative capacity?' or 'How does X's view of power differ from Y's?' This had the added benefit of honing my lecturing skills because I was forced to focus sharply on answering the question or explaining the concept.

I then tackled the problem of volume. Typing hundreds of responses was not a good idea and not typing them meant they were read too fleetingly. I found ways to limit the word count. For example, I would ask:

What did you learn today (3 points)?
In less than 10 words, comment on...
What are the first five words that pop into your mind when...?

Despite the obvious reduction in words, I was still faced with hundreds of responses. How might I give all students a voice without losing sleep? The light bulb went off above my head. The answer lay in my own research. I had just finished co-writing a book on random selection in politics and was preoccupied with the way in which random selection could lead to increased representativeness and, therefore, enhanced fairness in political decision making. It made sense to me to employ in the lecture hall the principles I was espousing in the political arena. The ocean liner was steadily moving to starboard. Students were now asked similar prompt questions to those that had been asked before, for example:

Something I need to understand better is…

What is one thing you learned in today's session?

What specifically needs to happen in the coming weeks for you to do well in this course?

However, they were also alerted to principles of fairness and the process of random selection as a tool to improve fairness. They were told that a random sample of their responses would be read and that these would be seen as representative of the group. Several methods were trialled. On occasions, all who wanted to would respond and I would read only some (for example every tenth response). On other occasions, I would invite, for example, only the third person from the end of every aisle or only the people in rows 10, 14 and 20. This worked very well and in the absence of contrary statements, the comments collected from a sample of about 10 per cent seemed to be representative of the whole.

There was a recurring theme when students were asked to comment on lectures and the following sums it up:

When you involve us during the lecture I am more likely to remain interested.

So the difficulty of interactivity remained. A common problem in governance is being able to encourage interactive deliberation amongst citizens and not just to offer an opportunity for simplistic yes/no responses of the kind that are extracted in opinion polls. Here was the problem being played out in the lecture hall. Though I used interactivity as an occasional tool in a one-hour lecture, I put my thinking cap on and designed a lecture that revolved completely around student interaction. Concurrently I was testing interactive consultation methods in the community and the response was very similar – highly enthusiastic. Here is what I did.

I wanted to look at power in relation to differing world views and perspectives. Rather than explaining to students how citizens adopt different perspectives in response to political issues, I used the entire lecture time as a role-playing exercise. The idea was borrowed from Joyce Stalker, an academic working in New Zealand. The lecture hall was divided into four groups and roles were distributed that conformed to four categories, ie consensus, conflict, New Right, postmodern. Every tenth student was issued with a statement that exemplified a particular perspective – some were purposely provocative. I used a controversial uranium mine as the case study. The class was highly interactive, with lots of passionate outbursts from those proclaiming views they did not actually believe. Others parroted the statements handed to them, then threw them away and demanded that their own view be heard. I recall standing in the middle of an aisle, high up the lecture hall, smiling, as amongst this huge group, learning was occurring, and democracy was breaking out. I was happy to have experimented with a teaching approach that could meet the challenges of this traditional lecture setting while maintaining my own values.

- Why do you think the strategies adopted were successful?
- What if any do you think are the limiting factors determining teaching methods that can be used in a traditional lecture setting?
- What are the implications for your own teaching raised by this case?

DISCUSSION

The difficulties of transplanting a system of reciprocal feedback into a large lecture format should not be underestimated. Many problems could not be overcome. The biggest problem was not to do with extracting feedback but how to respond to it. Students responded both positively and negatively to aspects of the course that proved to be impossible to change because of the course's tight structure and the alignment between the course objectives, lectures, tutorials, weekly readings and assessment. The promise of responsiveness to feedback could not always be delivered. For example, students identified that they would like alternate lectures to be used for the experiential format that was described earlier as well as using these alternate sessions as a commentary on each guest speaker's lecture. So every second lecture would review the one before in an interactive way. This was an excellent idea but one that could not be accommodated given the predetermined structure of the course.

In my research I had observed the need for 'contracting' in any community consultation and this, too, was evident in the lecture hall. In enacting participatory processes at any level of government, deep suspicion exists between citizens and politicians. This absence of trust can obstruct participatory processes. One effective way of dealing with this lack of trust is to establish a contract. When cynical citizens are drawn into a consultation process, they suspect that it will be tokenistic, that their input will be ignored – as it often is. However, if a governing authority states that it will act on citizens' recommendations, or agrees to state publicly why it does not do so, then citizens have far more confidence in the process.

Similarly in the large lecture setting it was important to make no false promises. Input could be considered and heeded only within the limitations of the course structure and timetable. If students are aware of this, their expectations for change are realistic and trust is not compromised. As with a governing authority, a lecturer needs to be very clear at the outset about the extent to which he or she can be responsive to students' feedback. Being told that a number of students have requested an outcome that cannot be met this semester but will influence the procedure for the following semester can still result in a degree of empowerment. But this will only occur if students know in advance what is possible.

Although I had wanted to give away some control of the classroom, in reality I was hampered by the structure and I could not give away as much power as I would have wished. I had wanted to step aside from the belief that I could or should be responsible for everything that goes on. Interestingly, feedback can reinforce the belief that what the student wants, the teacher gives. This was not my experience with reciprocal feedback, however, as the 'respectful listening' modelled in the teaching seemed to stimulate shared responsibility. If the teacher and students together identify areas of difficulty, together they can experiment until a solution is found.

A most useful discovery was the modified, random approach that made feedback more manageable and meaningful. It provided an accurate and useful guide to the group's overall learning. Students valued the opportunity to be heard and the chance to interact in a large group. They were mirroring the findings of my community research – that citizens above all else value good listening. Citizens are disgruntled by politicians who do not listen, just as students are by non-responsive lecturers. Politicians who are astute enough to share their power are judged favourably by empowered constituents just as lecturers are judged favourably by students whose power is unleashed.

Does size matter? Small groups can be collaborative, egalitarian and cemented with trust. The opposite is also true. Small groups can be extremely resistant to a democratic breakout and very prone to concentrations of power. It is perhaps not surprising then that large groups are just as contrary to any rule. A breakout in democracy in a large group can make one's toes curl. Maybe these eruptions of shared power are made more thrilling because they are unexpected and so difficult to achieve. Democracy can be exhilarating but also charged with anxiety and these experiments with shared responsibility were often as anxiety making for students in my lectures as they were for me. However, the ongoing feedback indicated that the struggle was worth it.

CHAPTER 15

CLEARLY, YOU CAN'T DO IT

Case reporter: Gina Wisker

ISSUES RAISED

This case study explores the challenge of teaching culturally sensitive material to a large group of students in a conventional lecture setting.

BACKGROUND

The case takes place in a UK university where an experienced female lecturer is teaching a large group of first-year students a module on contemporary poetry.

PART 1

I am a white middle-class female academic with a specialism in postcolonial and popular 20th century women's writing. This is one of my favourite areas of work – performance poetry largely by Afro-Caribbean and Black British poets. I have run seminars for a few years working with small groups of students on Black and Asian women's writing. I find that in the small groups students can become sensitive to cultural differences and aware of the very different oral history and context from which much writing by Black and Asian writers springs.

The first-year module is concerned with three contemporary poets. The first two are white and male, Tony Harrison and Thom Gunn, followed by an Afro-Caribbean/Black-British woman performance poet, Jean 'Binta' Breeze. The course aims to introduce students to different kinds of contemporary poetry as well as reading, enjoyment and analysis of poetry in a variety of forms.

The course takes the format of a weekly lecture to 150 students in a lecture theatre followed by a smaller seminar session. Students become used to this format, taking notes, discussing and reading the poems in class, then writing about them in a final essay. I really enjoy teaching this module because it can engage students in a variety of issues relating to the writing of poetry. I personally prefer the seminar to the lecture as it allows me to engage with the students in a developmental dialogue through the texts. A lecture is too large for this interaction, and it is difficult to gauge student responses in the same way. However, I felt that it was important to introduce the whole-year group to the issues and the practices of Black performance poetry in context.

The students who select this optional module choose to study and read the work of people from different cultural contexts. They are usually open to discussions about what kinds of cultural expectations we might have and if the Black and Asian writing might differ from this, or be similar to it. I try to avoid a 'them and us' situation in which writing from other cultural contexts appears strange and different, an anthropological specimen.

I start the seminar series by exploring cultural backgrounds. I do this in terms of where the students were born, where they have lived and travelled, where their parents come from and so on, and if they have experienced being part of a different cultural group amongst a majority. I explore some of their experiences with Black and Asian culture and writing, and some of their perceptions. This leads on to reading poetry, looking at images, and becoming involved in lots of discussion, helping students engage, reflect and move on.

This case was different. I knew that the lecture I was about to give had none of the advantages of the sensitive benefits of small-group work. I walked into the lecture theatre that morning full of enthusiasm and confidence, knowing that I could handle the cultural sensitivities and the dissonance between a very academic context and the enjoyment of performance poetry. After all, I had delivered parts of this content many times before. I was wrong!

I was met with a sea of expectant faces, the lecture room was full and as I started the lecture the buzz of conversations slowly died down. I certainly had their attention. I began with some comments about presenting and contextualizing writing which comes from different cultural contexts, and carefully used a range of eminent critics, most of them Black or Asian. These critics suggest we find out more about the cultural context of the work, and if it is from an oral culture, preferably hear it.

Unfortunately, Jean Breeze was not available on this Monday morning at 10. Yes, she really does give performances as part of the semester's literary activity! However, I pressed on. I discussed where real oral poetry has historically been found, movements from the Bards, the Mersey poets, Bob Dylan, the Beatles, to contemporary performance and oral work today. I set the cultural context of Afro-Caribbean-Black writing with some historical background. I delivered some poems or parts of poems by other white British performance poets and analysed them. It was not easy to do this in such a large auditorium and I really had to work hard at keeping the students attention.

I then read a poem by Jean Breeze. I thought the students would really enjoy this aspect. It was a mistake. I knew it as soon as I started. The students had that look on their face of 'Oh no how could she!' I tried not to look nervous, although underneath my bravado, I was trembling. To give myself the benefit of the situation, I decided to back up my reading with a taped version of the poet reading her own work. This seemed to work, so I continued and asked the students to turn to their neighbour and talk through what she was saying: language, references, rhyme, rhythm, speaking voice, imagery and so on. Students quickly engaged with the activity and there was a general buzz of conversation around the lecture theatre. Just as I was thinking I had 'saved the day' one of the students (a white female about 18 years old) came up onto the platform and said, 'I hope you are going to find a Black woman lecturer to give us these lectures because clearly you can't do it.'

- What do you think was really happening here?
- What do you think the lecturer did next?
- What would you do in a similar situation?

PART 2

As the lecture had now finished, the students slowly filtered out of the lecture theatre. I felt devastated, what had I done wrong? All that preparation – yes, the lecture had started well enough and just as I thought I had made some progress the blow came, and at full force.

Immediately I was aware that I had to handle this as a reasonable statement as well as one that shocked and surprised me. It was unusual for a student in the first year to be quite so forthright and I did not know whether this was normal behaviour for her or whether I had seriously upset her personally by working with Afro-Caribbean performance poetry. Perhaps it was not that I was doing it, but the way I was doing it.

An immediate reaction was to ask her why she felt that way, what the difficulty was, and to explain that indeed it might be more appropriate to have Black women academics presenting on Black women poets. However, this also assumes that anyone can only discuss someone else's work if he or she actually comes from an identical background and context. This would make Shakespeare equally difficult to work with! Sadly, we do not have a Black female literature academic at our university, so in a sense they were stuck with me. Nevertheless, as this is an area in which I work I felt it was important that students gain access to it. However, I did not share these thoughts with her.

I felt I needed to play for time, as I did not think I could give the student a reasoned and rational explanation. So, feeling a little cowardly, I thanked her for her comments and said I would get back to her. We both left the room and then I mulled it over.

I realized that I needed to calm down, as I could actually feel myself shaking. A hot cup of coffee would help me to think through some of the issues more clearly. Now in the calm and security of my office I reflected on the lecture and the student who had caused me so much pain.

It is difficult to work with material from another cultural context. However, if we do not, students might not meet this work. This would deprive them of some fine and very different work – in this case poetry (it could be true of art, performance, music and probably many other subjects and areas too). If we only relied on staff from the cultures whose work we are discussing, then we would limit access to that work since universities are unlikely to have such a huge range of staff.

I asked myself was it the lack of authenticity and accent that caused the comment. Maybe I had not given a good performance. I continued to think about the issues and it occurred to me that one answer might be to ask one of my Black colleagues in. However, they do not work in literature, and it would be rather absurd to centre-stage a colleague from the same cultural context as the poet but who teaches health, for example, and expect her to comment. It might also be insulting, as if every Black person could speak for every other Black person.

I still thought it crucial to lay the ground carefully not only regarding the cultural context and where the work comes from, but also the whole argument about access to this work. We should have access but not try to take it over. This is an issue with interpreting all creative work of course, but with that from a different cultural context it becomes laced with the potential for a new form of cultural imperialism, taking over, labelling, dismissing?

I did not think this was being too sensitive. I could use some of the statements from Black and Asian critics who say we have a right to read and enjoy work in writing from different contexts. Highlighting the issues would enable the students to be more reflective. I found some postcolonial critics who articulated similar arguments and put it in their words, 'you should be angry with a history which has so silenced you…' (says one critic, while another argues we must read Black writing but that White people can speak *about* but never *for* Black people).

Performance poetry relies on the interaction between the performer who owns the poetry and the audience who share it and partly make it work. It is difficult to mimic or model this situation when working with someone else's poetry. Certainly, my lecture on this Monday morning was no replacement for the open air, or a pub or wherever the performance usually takes place.

Still, working hard at finding a solution, I set out to find the poets in performance and to let them speak for themselves. This meant very careful monitoring of available videos and of TV performance extracts, of taped work, and of matching the poems themselves to the visual or oral presentation that I found (and which could be reproduced in copyright terms!). Apart from a few poems with which I felt safe, not those that were in the vernacular or everyday speech and not those that relied upon particular pronunciation impossible for me to model, students now hear and see the poets themselves, rather than me.

Oddly, the next year one of the students came up and said – was I saying that she could not read the poems aloud for herself because I was not reading them aloud? Maybe we need to be careful when we are put in 'a performance situation' and one where we could be seen to try to represent or speak *for* instead *of* poets from a different cultural context.

It has struck me since that it is much easier to enlist people to read aloud, to hear the students work with the poetry from different cultural contexts and to articulate their own concerns about doing so, when we do this in a small group. This enables sensitive sharing and discussion of issues which worry students, or which certainly worried this particular student.

In my smaller groups trust and familiarity, experimentation and sharing enabled more exciting immediate and risky activities, as well as a shared discussion of how we deal with difficulties. The smaller seminar space is ideal, but since we have the lecture theatre and lecture format, we have to work with it as best we can. Now that same lecture is a more manageable and sensitive experience and is certainly a much more hi-tech, more authentic experience!

- Would you have acted differently?
- Are there any comparisons of sensitivity and appropriateness in your own subject area that could produce these difficulties?

DISCUSSION

My case raises issues of who has authority to present and engage with material that is culturally sensitive. How can we go about making such material available in a way that does not seem to appropriate or steal it, take it over, yet does enable us to engage with it critically? It asks questions about how we can empower students to find their own voice in relation to material and ideas that effectively challenge some of their own cultural assumptions. There are some issues raised with looking at any poet – their context, the kind of poetic choices they make, how poetry works generally to enable poets and readers to engage with emotions, experiences, expressions and arguments through sound, pattern, language and so on. But there are specific issues raised by teaching and writing from a culture quite different from one's own.

My experience raised the issue about how a conventional lecture setting can enable such interactions with sensitive and stimulating material in a way that allows it to stay alive, enabling students to engage immediately with the real material rather than a second- or third-hand representation of it. It was important to me for students to engage analytically and imaginatively, not merely to experience the material.

There are also several learning dimensions to this case. The context of a large lecture group is one issue, since what can be taught and learned within a large class is restricted by the kinds of interaction possible in that context. Lecturers cannot teach with direct interaction with each student as one might in a seminar. Also there will be a diversity of student learning conceptions and approaches. Staff cannot know these different needs and styles beforehand.

Research carried out on student learning in large classes suggests that students are more engaged in learning processes when they are given the opportunity to be actively involved. This was what I was trying to do. I wanted to give students the opportunity to listen, to see and to read work by the performance poets. I wanted to give a performance to help that learning. I also wanted students to discuss their work, in pairs or threes, giving them an opportunity to be active learners within the session.

According to Kolb (1998), learning activities related to experience are more likely to be integrated with students' previous learning and with their lifelong learning. In the case of my work with performance and Afro-Caribbean poetry, integrating experience and lifelong learning was crucial.

Students also need to consider how we can deal with products of different cultures in a non-culturally imperialist way. They need to learn to respond to the different techniques, language and meanings of such texts in ways that do not immediately privilege the established canon of white middle-class writers. Instead, there is a need to recognize contexts and cultures that produce performance and oral work. By utilizing video and oral replay students were able to experience the affective domain of the work with Black and Asian writing. Seminar work that follows can then offer guidance, interpretation and encourage questions on the issues raised, thus engaging students in a 'critical' activity.

Another issue is that of the student who came up onto the platform. Students are rarely so confident that they can directly approach a member of staff with the problem they perceive in a large-scale situation like a lecture. I would not want students to feel that they could not address such problems. However, not every student would feel able to make such a direct approach. I felt it was abrasive, but I would not want to try to close it down. Such discussions would be better carried on in a small group than at a lecture. Perhaps if someone did disrupt with such an issue it would be appropriate to suggest he or she discuss it later in the seminar. In this case, the student did not disrupt the lecture. (She certainly disrupted me! But that is not the real point.)

Many of us have to deal with sensitive material and with affective or change-oriented learning outcomes. It is a wise decision to deal with these sensitively and preferably in a small group, where thoughts can be aired. However, if it has to be done in a large group, then simulating the sharing, the contextualizing, the critical issues and then the work itself is important.

REFERENCES

Kolb, D A (1998) Learning styles and disciplinary differences, in *Teaching and Learning in the College Classroom*, ed K A Feldman and M B Paulsen, pp 151–64, Simon and Schuster, Needham Heights, Massachusetts

CHAPTER 16

How can i lecture that topic?

Case reporter: Joy Higgs

ISSUES RAISED

This case focuses on the difficulty of planning a lecture programme to teach a topic that is best learned from experience, by 'doing' and seeking to understand, rather than by being 'told'.

BACKGROUND

An experienced physiotherapy educator has been invited to teach the topic of clinical reasoning to a group of 15 coursework students taking a masters degree in manipulative physiotherapy in an Australian university. The students are mature age, graduate physiotherapists studying in a specialist clinical studies programme part time, and attending a two-week residential course.

PART 1

How should I go about planning this course on clinical reasoning? I reflected that it would be easy to plan several traditional lectures and leave time for questions, then pack up and go home. But that would not do justice to the audience, topic, desired outcomes or context.

For instance, I knew from previous experience that the students are typically experienced clinicians seeking to develop advanced clinical knowledge and skills. There is a tradition of competition amongst them. They are seeking to succeed in a competitive clinical marketplace that makes them keen to excel and to display strengths rather than limitations in their clinical and/or learning abilities. For example, a student once said to me:

When I began the clinical reasoning class it was very stressful. In all my other subjects I was getting high distinction grades. Here, hard work just wasn't enough. I had to dig down into myself. Why was I sure this was the correct diagnosis or treatment? And, I wasn't allowed to say 'Isn't it obvious?' or 'The literature says…' I had to unravel my thinking and come up with a rationale that was justified and articulate. Many times I knew that I knew – but didn't want to say something that sounded stupid or was wrong.

This was my first challenge: how could I facilitate the development/ enhancement of clinical reasoning abilities when the students were likely to be inhibited from displaying their learning needs and difficulties?

I remembered another conversation, this time with a colleague in the tea room before we began teaching a clinical reasoning programme:

Look, what's the big deal? We've all learned to reason on the job. Why devote two whole subjects to clinical reasoning? Let the students pick it up during clinical education placements. Leave it up to the clinical educators to quiz them a bit on their reasoning. It's the treatment techniques that really count anyway. That's why the students come back for postgraduate study.

So here was my second dilemma: can clinical reasoning be taught at all?

My own research and experience suggests that it can (eg Higgs and Jones, 2000). The traditional practice in health sciences curricula has been to teach clinical problem solving, the overt acts associated with reasoning (such as planning treatments), which can be recorded in the patient's history. However, such processes have the appearance, not the complexity or deep substance of reasoning. Curricula have tended to rely too much on experience alone to 'fill in the gaps' in the problem-solving process and I also wanted to blend adult and self-reflective learning with exploration of clinical reasoning.

Finally, I wanted to adopt an approach that recognized the professional artistry in reasoning as well as teaching. The concept of professional artistry as applied to clinical practice is seen by some as non-scientific, unsubstantial and 'pre-professional', reflecting an era when practice relied on accumulated experience and trial and error, rather than on the 'more solid foundations' of empirical analytical research.

My own background had led me to see clinical reasoning as a blending of such artistry with the science which underpins clinical practice, the craft which emerges through clinical practice, the ethical behaviour learned through life and professional teachings, and the care and humanity which we endeavour to enhance rather than annihilate during professional education and practice. And inherent in the performance of skilled clinical reasoners is an exquisite capacity for professional judgement (a term that I prefer to the broader notion of intuition) grounded in a deep, rich, constantly evolving professional knowledge base.

I wanted to create a learning programme where the students engaged directly with the challenges encompassed in the exploration of clinical reasoning. I wanted to face the exciting and demanding 'collision' of the scientific medical model and the emerging clinical and teaching trends of professional artistry and metacognitive practice. All of this represented no small task. How should I proceed?

- What do you think would be an ideal way of teaching this course?
- Could such a course be taught through lectures?
- What do you think the lecturer actually did?

PART 2

A call came from the programme coordinator: 'Just phoning to discuss your two days in the masters programme… we're drawing up the pre-residential information and I wanted to check on the titles of your lectures…'

'Lectures?… You want me to teach this programme by lectures?!' Well there is an interesting dilemma. At least the venue was not a tiered lecture theatre. I needed to have some high-grade combustible interaction going on in this programme!

After the call I reflected on my own experiences of sitting through lectures:

- 10-year-old packaged lectures where the presenter is twice as bored as the audience;
- high-powered and highly paced expressions of the presenter's self-aggrandisement without consideration of learners' readiness or interest;
- inspirational journeys to the heart of what becomes a life-long fascination;
- slick high-tech performances where the message is drowned in the 'wow' of the presentation technique;
- clearly structured presentations seeking to promote understanding.

I began to think that what I needed was a bit of creative reframing. What if I considered a lecture as a mode of teaching in which a group (large or small) of students participate in the learning of content through the presentation of material, engagement of the learners in understanding and evaluating the content, and promotion of learners' perceptions of relevance of that content to their learning needs? That sounded flexible enough! But how best could I plan a two-day programme using this interactive lecture-presentation approach?

I drew on three goals and experiences to address this task: my desire for the students to be active and interactive, my experience with similar programmes which led to a supportive yet challenging approach, and my goal of helping the students 'get inside' the science, skill and artistry of clinical reasoning. The glue to hold all of this together was a strategy to work from an overall plan, a teaching framework, and to unfold and adapt this during the teaching programme through the art of metacognitive teaching. I designed a programme comprising six hours of lecture presentations and five hours of clinical reasoning practical sessions involving the discussion of hypothetical clinical cases. The practical sessions focused on students' exploration and articulation of their reasoning.

My classes were at the beginning of the second week of a two-week residential programme for the master's degree. Most of the previous week had concentrated on the acquisition and testing of practical skills and lectures on biomedical/clinical topics. So, my classes would be rather a change of pace.

I had arrived the night before but could not access the venue until the morning. The classroom was a large multipurpose room set up with clinical treatment beds at one end and chairs in rows (mini-lecture format) at the others. My first task was to arrange the chairs in a horseshoe shape to promote student discussion opportunities. I was anticipating a polite audience, keen to learn, if somewhat unenthused to be moving away from more familiar clinical topics. I knew the mode of teaching would be challenging to their expectations of 'receptive student mode' and 'teacher talk'. The seating arrangement as I arrived indicated a previous week of practical classes and standard lectures. I knew that turning on the overhead projector would be the signal for 'pick up your pens and start writing'. I needed to switch this to 'time to start thinking'. I began the class as follows:

> Welcome to the class. Over the next two days we're going to explore the topic of clinical reasoning – what we know about this from the perspective of theory and research – and more importantly what you know about it from your clinical experience. Would each of you introduce yourself and tell the group what you understand by the term clinical reasoning, and how you use reasoning in your practice.

Each person was encouraged to talk about his or her experiences with brief encouraging verbal and non-verbal feedback provided to recognize both their comments and their 'courage' in revealing their knowledge and thinking. We negotiated goals and the programme, within a broad framework I provided, linked to key topics in clinical reasoning theory, research and practice. This exercise started to set the scene for what I knew were the challenges that lay ahead. So far, the atmosphere was pleasant, friendly and cooperative.

The morning alternated between input, questions and buzz groups. The latter were particularly useful to loosen up the climate and increase comfortable participation. As the interaction continued it was good to recognize that passive note taking by the students was completely absent, and at the same time, the volume of talk during buzz group sessions showed enthusiasm and enjoyment.

Later evaluations included the following comments:

> I came expecting the usual talk and chat – this was really different. From the first moment we had to do a lot of thinking. It was challenging but fascinating.
>
> I really liked the way our knowledge and experience was used. I felt that my clinical experience was being valued. And, it was surprising to me how much I actually knew.

After the lunch break we switched to the topic of knowledge underpinning and derived from clinical practice:

> The goal of this session is to explore your existing knowledge bases; to do a self-diagnostic if you like. I'd like you to brainstorm individually for five minutes – write down everything you know about (... unfamiliar, allocated clinical condition). Now, choose a clinical condition that you are very familiar with and write down everything you know about it. (5 minutes).

These individual brainstorms were used to provide the content and links for cognitive maps. The students individually drew their maps on large sheets of newsprint. We spent time admiring the artwork and discussing the quality, depth and extent of their knowledge, and the difficulties in taking knowledge that is often used invisibly in reasoning and 'unbundling' it and making it explicit. Students gave mini-presentations on their knowledge using the cognitive maps as a framework.

The later evaluations again told the story:

> I was astonished at how much I knew and how much knowledge I rely on in my practice. It was liberating to hear (and believe it) that the knowledge from my experience was valid. I really liked looking at the research models which showed that clinical expertise involves a high level of knowledge from practice as well as theory and research.
>
> I was quite astonished at how hard it was to talk about my knowledge and how much of my knowledge was patchy and incomplete. I thought I knew it – but I'm just starting to find out how much more I need to learn – not just cramming for the knowledge tests – but really knowing things well enough to explain my clinical reasoning and decisions.

On day two we moved more into the practice of clinical reasoning. This was to be a riskier topic because we would challenge students' comfortable assumptions and confidence by asking questions such as 'What is the basis for that conclusion/decision?', 'What would you expect the results of that test/intervention to be and why?'

The lecture presentations focused on the implications and necessity of clinical reasoning competence in the light of the responsibilities and privilege of physiotherapists working as primary contact practitioners, particularly those in private practice. The students were asked to deal with the uncertainty of practice, the greyness (as well as the illuminating strength) of knowledge and the need to abandon the learned role of knowledgeable clinician who prescribes and administers treatments to passive, compliant patients. They confronted their habits, the community's expectations and the realities they would face if they were physiotherapy clients. Models of patient-centred care, self-help, the wellness model and client-focused primary care became inspiring, if demanding, topics of debate.

More evaluations:

We debated the topic of the patient's role in clinical decision making. There were several opposing viewpoints – support for patient compliance versus informed consent and self-responsibility. For the first time these became real practices, not just ideas or definitions. Putting myself into the patient's role really made me think about how I treat my patients. I'm going to try to adopt a more partnership approach to clinical practice in the future.

We really talked about multicultural communities and how the changing mix of patients we work with means that we need to change our approaches – to learn how to interact better with people where they are coming from.

Day two also saw the introduction of 'hypotheticals-fish bowl' sessions where we discussed clinical cases based on realistic but hypothetical conditions and contexts. Several students actively discussed the case with expert and peer critique of their knowledge and reasoning. For experienced clinicians this is a threatening experience because the countless bits of taken-for-granted knowledge, the 'logic' of clinical reasoning and the assumptions and knowledge which underlie the reasoning process are taken out of the invisible, non-conscious realm of rapid and individual reasoning, and scrutinized by self, peers and teachers.

For myself, this latter part of the two days, after the group had warmed up, had gained trust in one another and had learned to 'say foolish, tentative or absolutely brilliant things to each other', was both demanding and exciting. It was demanding, because it was my job to create just enough threat – not too much, just enough comfort – but with a dash of unsettling spice, and enough student self-revelation – but not embarrassment. It meant being constantly on my toes handling the multiple levels of the reasoning task alongside the complex interpersonal, learning and feedback dimensions of the task.

For the students it was a mixture of 'I hope it's not my turn next', 'I thought I knew that', 'She'll ask me a question and I won't be able to remember a thing' and 'Wow, I guess I know more than I realized'. The room at afternoon teatime was filled with these words and with a buzz of raised awareness as well as raised tension – a rather nice mix of both.

From a background of limited communication of reasoning and little emphasis on this aspect of clinical practice in their education to date, this session was a new experience for the students. As a result of the interactive lecture-presentation, the students came to appreciate the nature of clinical reasoning and they reported gaining greater confidence in being able to examine their own knowledge and reasoning. For example, they commented as follows:

I was wondering what on earth we were going to spend two days on. You know – clinical reasoning – you just do it. So it was quite a revelation to think about all the research that's been going on. I came away enthusiastic to learn more about it.

We worked really hard the whole two days, rather than just sitting there. There was a variety of different activities and each one made us think or reflect in a new way.

I learned a lot about myself and how I think about clinical practice. It's given me a new way of understanding clinical decision making. And I took away a list of topics where I need to brush up my knowledge. But this was a positive outcome – not a feeling of failure.

- What do you think about the approach taken?
- Do you agree that 'lecturing' can be seen as an activity within an overall programme rather than a 'thing' itself?
- Could the approach taken have worked with a larger group or in a different subject area?
- Are there any areas of overlap between this case and your own teaching?

DISCUSSION

My experiences as a teacher of teachers and as a teacher of health professionals has led me to develop and appreciate four lenses for viewing teaching and learning. The first of these is the use of strategies for helping to develop students' self-direction (Higgs, 1993). The conundrum to be faced here is to create controlled freedom: to provide sufficient structure of an appropriate type to match the learner's readiness for the task. Secondly, there is the need to develop professional artistry, bringing one's unique artistic interpretation to teaching; blending individual qualities, skills and creative imagination. Third is the need to develop process-inclusive curricula (Everingham and Bandaranayake, 1999) that deliberately target, exemplify and depict the processes of thinking and reasoning as core values, goals and learning outcomes. Finally, metacognitive teaching refers to the act of teaching from a prepared educational and philosophical stance, utilizing a rich knowledge base of the subject area and employing such skills during teaching to harness this knowledge and be true to the stance adopted.

For me, teaching then is a mixture of art, craft and science. In reflecting on these approaches, I am conscious of parallels with Kolb's (1984) learning cycle that seems to me to have a special magic of widespread relevance to many situations. In craft mode we are 'up to our ears' in concrete experience and active experimentation, the being and doing of our trade. In the science/theory approach to teaching, we focus heavily on abstract conceptualization or thinking acts with a dash of experimentation thrown in for good measure. In art, reflective observation or feeling predominates; the essence of appreciation lies in the artist's critical reflection during the artistic creation and in the audience's observations of the created artwork. In the fullest sense of professional artistry, however, we combine all of these skills and processes.

So how were these approaches manifest in this case? Firstly, in terms of promoting the students' self-direction, the programme was a framework guided by me but shaped also by the students. In this way, they helped to create their own programme. This is illustrated by the following student comment:

> I liked the way we practised self-direction as well as talking about it. For instance, we spent quite some time looking at our own knowledge and reasoning skills, identifying individual targets to address during the course and afterwards. We were able to participate in the design of the overall programme and to make suggestions for changing the programme to address our learning needs. I felt that I was able (along with my fellow students) to shape the course to help me to learn.

In the end, all of the lecture-presentations I had prepared were used. I varied the content to adapt to the students' background knowledge and responses, and, of course, their input was very much individual and unpredicted. The richness and shape of the final product of this approach was a joint effort. Of the other activities, we spent much longer than I had tentatively planned on the mind-mapping session. The students' interest was intense and they opted for an additional hour on this activity rather than moving on to the next lecture-presentation (which was subsequently shortened from two hours to one).

The framework for the course was pre-planned to move from orientation, confidence building, affirmation of prior learning, through exploration of new material (theory and research on clinical reasoning), to build on this with practical exploration of the concepts/theory and their own reasoning, and ending in reflection and self-evaluation. This overall framework was implemented as planned. The differences resulting from the students' input were in re-apportioning time and emphasis. In addition, the group, being largely cohesive and supportive from previous learning together, was able to move quickly into the more challenging phase of the programme. This allowed more time to be spent on self and peer exploration of clinical reasoning in action.

Second, the process-inclusive curriculum was realized in that the more we talked about the nature of clinical reasoning in emerging models of health care, the more the parallels between the teaching model we were aspiring to co-create and the clinical practice partnership model we were exploring became apparent. Third, professional artistry overlapped both the content and the process of this learning programme. It was one of my goals to illustrate how clinical reasoning was a multidimensional factor bringing together art, craft, science, humanity and ethics. We talked about these dimensions in the class, we practised them in the clinical reasoning hypotheticals and we paused from time to time to articulate examples of professional artistry clearly, when these became apparent.

Finally, the skill of metacognitive teaching is essential to achieve the targets above. During the classes, I processed, monitored and adjusted my thinking constantly. I kept in touch with my goals and lenses, as well as with the action playing out around and with me. My final advice to anyone attempting this type of teaching is to remember self-preservation. The heightened awareness and being constantly on your toes can be quite tiring. So, start slowly and pace yourself. My colleagues and I have found it is desirable (for ourselves and the students) to share the role of 'orchestra conductor' in two-hour classes. This form of interactive lecture-presentation is certainly more demanding than a straightforward lecture. But I have found it to be rewarding and empowering.

REFERENCES

Everingham, F and Bandaranayake, R (1999) Teacher education programmes for health science educators, in *Educating Beginning Practitioners: Challenges for health professional education*, ed J Higgs and H Edwards, Butterworth Heinemann, Oxford, pp 263–70

Higgs, J (1993) The teacher in self-directed learning: Manager or co-manager? in *Learner Managed Learning: Practice, theory and policy*, ed N J Graves, World Education Fellowship, London, pp 122–31

Higgs, J and Jones, M (ed) (2000) *Clinical Reasoning in the Health Professions*, 2nd edn, Butterworth Heinemann, Oxford

Kolb, D A (1984) *Experiential Learning – Experience as the source of learning and development*, Prentice-Hall Inc, New Jersey

CHAPTER 17

FROM BIG WATER TO REFLECTIVE POOLS

Case reporters: William M Timpson and Bill G Wright

ISSUES RAISED

The issues raised by this case study relate to the use of small collaborative study/learning groups in large lecture classes.

BACKGROUND

The case occurred in a large US university. Two groups of students were involved. The first group was a first-year class making the transition to university and taught by Bill. The second group was a large introductory zoology class taught by William. Both Bill and William were concerned about lack of student involvement in lectures and their feelings of isolation, neglect and the lack of group identity.

PART 1

Have you ever found yourself hurtling down a river boiling with rapids and white water? Was it fun? Terrifying? Or found yourself moving slowly, inexorably down a mighty river? The differences are obvious and immense. What follows is a case study in collaboration and parallel exploration of the use of small study groups in large lecture classes. We use the river analogy to frame our experiences of using turbulent small groups in ponderous large lecture classes to promote more active, more engaged and deeper student learning.

I (Bill) teach a large introductory zoology class. I also do basic research. I cannot spend too much time on classroom issues without committing academic suicide. I love basic research as much as I love to teach and I cannot conceive of one without the other. So although my time budget is heavily constrained, I want students to learn more in my class than in any of their other classes. The question for me then is 'How can I give the kayak keys to my students and send them up the tributary, more or less on their own.'

I (William) teach a large lecture class of first-year students making the transition to university. While I have the benefit of discussion sections, I want to make the most of my time and explore new possibilities.

Both of us were concerned that students were coming to lectures with little enthusiasm or willingness to answer questions or engage in discussion. Also, we know students feel isolated from one another, especially in a very large university. After years of experience with teaching large lecture courses and much exploration on our own, we wanted to explore the benefits of alternative routes. Journeys onto smaller bodies of water, where the flow is more navigable, where exploring pools allows students deeper reflections, where navigating small eddies permits some practice with skills needed for their own journeys down-river, where travellers get to venture out into the medium itself without risking their lives.

The 'enlightenment' came during one of Bill's office hour sessions. Rather than deal with students one at a time, Bill normally invites all students who come to his office door to join the group (3–8 students usually). The session that day following the lecture was typical – they asked Bill questions and he taught them directly the secrets of zoology. The ideal learning situation – low student–teacher ratio, motivated students. Piece of cake, right? Wrong!

A student can look me in the eye while being taught about segregation of gametes during meiosis, or the change in sodium conductance during the action potential. I teach them step by step, drawing on my enthusiasm, training and experience. Then I sit back and ask them to explain what they just learned. It is embarrassing to the extreme to admit how often they cannot do that. That day was no exception. The group was asked to explain the concept I had been talking about and I was met with a sea of blank faces. Susan cast her eyes to the floor as if a special zoological exhibit was there. Dee looked out of the window, carefully avoiding my glance. I sighed in desperation.

Are these students really so lacking in intelligence? Have they not listened to what I have been saying? Do they have other things on their mind? Or is it me? Have I done something wrong? I thought I explained things clearly and at the right pace – but clearly something is wrong. I thought that I must try to keep my cool and not show how disappointed I was in their lack of understanding – stamping my feet and going into a rage would not help anyone. I decided to go for a walk and leave the students in the room for a little while by themselves. This would give me an opportunity to calm down and clear my head, as I had so many negative thoughts.

- Have you had a similar experience of teaching and students not learning?
- Why do you think the students in this case had not learned?
- What would you have done when you got back to the room?
- What do you think Bill did?

PART 2

I returned to the room determined to be calm and to explain the concept again. I was not looking forward to this and expected to receive a somewhat hostile reaction from the students. I could tell they too had been feeling fraught and unhappy about their lack of understanding. However, on returning to the room, and much to my surprise I was warmly greeted by the students who were now smiling! So what had happened? Had someone announced some good news? Had they organized a party for that evening?

No, upon stepping further into the room I was greeted by 'now we understand'! Steve explained that he had understood but did not want to show himself up in front of me. However, as soon as I had left the room he explained the concept to the others in the way that he had understood it. He had tackled the problem from a different angle, and surprise surprise, they understood. So, what had actually happened whilst I was away? Was it that the students had learned in a small group where they could trust one another and did not feel embarrassed about admitting they did not understand? This did not happen in a large group lecture group where they were afraid of showing themselves up in front of their peers.

I discussed this with William and we both agreed to experiment with using smaller groups in our large lecture classes. We talked to colleagues over coffee. We also engaged a few students in one-to-one conversations, asking them what was different about being a member of a small group. Feedback told us that students felt more secure in small groups and able to admit when they did not understand the material.

So how could we apply this situation to some of our larger groups? We had both been intrigued with study and small project groups as viable antidotes to the challenges presented by lecturing to large groups of students. How could we use the learning from the 'office session' to enhance our lecturing? Could we make use of small groups within or related to the lecture? The challenge was to find the right mix of attention to process and product, spending time on the concepts and skills students need to work effectively in leaderless groups or focusing directly on course content. We also realized that getting more active student learning in a lecture class means attentiveness to these areas not usually explored, an alertness to opportunity, some willingness to explore, and to offer some training to students in the skills needed to guide their own learning boats. Could large classes become less isolating as students interact with peers, work through assignments and support one another's learning? Ultimately, could students come to lectures more energized, with new questions from their own explorations?

- How would you go about introducing small-group work into a large lecture class?
- How would you form the groups? What kind of activities would you give them?
- What do you think would be the major problems you would have to overcome?

PART 3

We decided to try two different approaches. First, Bill initiated the formation of small groups (3–6 students) working collaboratively and designed a series of problems that were to be solved by these groups outside of the formal lecture. These assignments were themselves directly linked to upcoming exams. Thus students benefited in two ways: nominal extra credit for handing in the completed task, and a hot line to the next exam, which is filled with the information they researched in their group tasks. Students were assigned (randomly) to groups of six, but they could strike their name from that group and add it to a different group. They could also choose not to be in a group. These individuals were welcome to take the assignment home and work on it on their own, but this option proved much less productive than when individuals in the group each took a section of the problem to conquer and brought their insights back to the group meeting.

Bill watched that first chaotic group formation; he still felt unsure that this was going to work. It took about a half an hour after one lecture. Groups were very fluid at first. Friendships and alliances were being made everywhere. The noise was deafening, but 60 per cent of the students signed into a group. The groups were assigned a weekly task relating directly to the lecture. These tasks usually represented a concept that the students had traditionally shown difficulty understanding. Some of the tasks were easier than others; some served the singular purpose of keeping the groups together.

Two-thirds of the class participated. The group members decided where and when to meet to discuss the weekly task. One of the assignments was for the groups to meet and choose one concept covered in lectures with which they had the most difficulty. The rewards were two-fold. The one obvious reward for Bill was the feedback provided from his students. The second was developing students' decision-making skills. Because they were allowed only one lecture topic to hand in, group members had to agree among themselves what that topic would be. Group members then had to complete the assignment by trying to explain the concepts to one another. This group-study project promoted active participation in comprehending the material and students worked within a group, regardless of their academic position within the class.

The results were impressive and the 'extra learning' was not just restricted to what students did in the small groups as much was also 'carried over' into the lecture. Students became more confident and were able to ask questions that previously they would have had difficulty asking. They also seemed to 'gel' more as a group and actually seemed to enjoy the lecture. We have seen increased exam performance for those participating and much greater student attentiveness in class. Our time in the lecture became more animated as more students came to class with questions that had grown out of their time together on the assignments. In turn, Bill found himself more animated, buoyed by greater student engagement and interest. Learning was becoming a more dynamic and interactive process and less of a passive student response to transmitted information by the lecturer.

The trade-off between process and product, between formal content coverage and more student-centred emphases on cooperative learning, has been largely successful and in the right direction. While we have been disappointed with lower than expected retention rates, our students' academic performance has surpassed a statistically matched control group and proven no worse than the overall first-year population despite a sizeable disadvantage in entering test scores and high-school grade point average. Moreover, the qualitative data we have collected and analysed have been encouraging, giving clear indications of more active student learning, more initiative, real skill development and, we think, a deeper understanding of underlying principles.

William was caught up in the enthusiasm of Bill's success with small groups and decided to lead a team of faculty, staff and graduate students in designing a new course to support first-year students in making a successful transition to the university. The course, 'Learning and Community', is intended to provide students with a deep understanding of learning, critical and creative thinking, communication, group dynamics and teamwork within our shared environment. William wanted students first to evaluate themselves as learners, to understand their strengths and address their weaknesses. He also wanted students to evaluate themselves as group members in the various communities to which they belonged. The idea is that with some greater understanding of themselves as learners, these students could function at a much higher level in our lectures, asking better questions, taking more initiative and handling more complex concepts and issues.

To support the programme, William wrote self-study materials for students and any lecturers who agreed to use this content. So a chemist, for example, could supplement formal content with attention to the ideas and skills students would need to work more effectively alone or in teams. William also worked with colleagues to develop and trial a new book, *Stepping Up: College learning and community* (Timpson, 1999). Specific topics included group learning and interdependence, communication, trust building, setting goals and resolving conflicts.

In cooperative learning and, in particular, in the development of study groups, we wanted students to learn about functional, healthy, supportive and sustainable communities and then take the initiative to form a voluntary study group in at least one of their lectures. We expected students to meet regularly with classmates to provide assistance to one another and support in meeting course requirements. If one attempt at forming a study group were to fail, we expected these students to assess what occurred and begin another group. So not only were we teaching them how to interact in groups for lectures, we were encouraging them to take what they learn out on the road and use it in their other classes.

To assess the impact of the course, we collected various traditional measures of student performance, including high-school scores, pre-enrolment and academic probation rates. We compared the performance of students in the three lectures – autumn 1997, 1998 and 1999 – with control groups matched on the admissions prediction index and with the general first-year student population on this campus. We conducted a formal end-of-semester assessment using the standard university student course survey as well as a more formative assessment at mid-semester using the same instrument. We also conducted a follow-up survey of graduates of this course.

So far, the data have been very encouraging. On quantitative measures of grades in college, our students have outperformed a statistically matched group, although the differences were not significant. Contrary to what we hoped, retention rates were nearly identical to those for the matched control group. However, our emphasis on values clarification and critical thinking suggests that course content may have helped some students make informed and thoughtful decisions about leaving the university. The initiative and creativity required of students to create functional study groups may have contributed to this kind of insight.

The most positive evidence about the course has come in response to a follow-up survey of those still enrolled. We asked for feedback about their experiences on campus. For members of the first class in 1997, over 50 per cent have attributed their success on campus generally to what they had learned in our course. Again, the study group requirement may have extended what had proven successful on a voluntary basis, ie students who naturally formed study groups outperformed those who did not.

In general, our students seemed to clarify their values as they increased their understanding about the benefits of active learning. For example, one student described unexpected benefits of her perseverance with a study group despite a number of recurring frustrations:

For an economics test, I got together with a couple of other guys to prepare for it. I had to explain this one concept to this guy about fifty times. It bothered me then, but really helped me later. Teaching him really made me learn the methods and concepts really well.

Our students seemed to have grown in their appreciation for their own initiative. For instance, one student found herself taking the initiative to facilitate a study group with upper-division students:

> I was a little nervous taking the leadership role because I was the little freshman who had no idea what was going on in class... Personally, I have found that the study group has put confidence into my studies... Because of the positive outcomes of this (course) project I have started two other small study groups with an environmental conservation course as well as my recreation course.

Our students also reported success from soliciting peer assistance, feedback and support. For example, one student athlete wrote:

> I gained a lot of awareness and upgraded my study habits... The (group members) helped me take my grade from an 'F' to a 'B'. This really helped my self-esteem and made me proud of myself.

We are encouraged by our assessments to date, in particular that students can deepen their understanding about themselves as learners and how they can make the most of the rich resources available to them at university.

DISCUSSION

In the context of an increasingly diverse campus community, cooperative groups represent one way to link individual student efforts so that they can assist and support one another's learning. As the lecturer, you also get to interact with students on a smaller, more personal scale. By grouping students with different abilities, backgrounds and viewpoints in such a way that they share ideas, you can accomplish much more than content coverage. When managed effectively, groups provide a social foundation that can help students develop skills in thinking critically and creatively. Lessons learned from cooperating with others in group activities also have value within and beyond classes and the campus.

We wondered how students would take to working in small groups, as our colleagues were very sceptical. One colleague thought groups were a waste of time, and that if students did not learn in lectures it was their fault. We also talked to some students who felt that there would be little benefit from groups. One particular student, Claire, did not want to join a group, she believed she could learn more by herself. However, with a little persuading, she agreed to try it and much to her surprise she actually enjoyed it. We found generally that students really enjoyed working in these small groups. Friendships were formed. Life in and around the courses relaxed a notch. Students got a unique angle on the material that seemed to result in real learning. It seemed that when students had to explain a concept, they were forced into an active mode. This active learning breaks down all kinds of learning barriers. Students got some 'feel' for teaching – those students in Bill's office had started to teach themselves. And we sense a distinctly increased enthusiasm about the class.

Alternatively, we could just give them the keys to the kayak and let them go. Granted, some would get stuck and give up. Students' social skills in introductory classes are typically widely divergent. Clearly, attentive management of these groups by the lecturer will improve their effectiveness. However, even without such management, these groups still perform a vast service, which is to tap into the ability of students to learn from and to teach one another. This was clearly demonstrated when students explained concepts to other group members.

Learning groups represent a powerful supplement to the traditional lecture format. By augmenting large lectures with small cooperative group activities, we share some of the responsibility for teaching with students. Our students become more active and engaged with the course material, participating in ways that we did not think possible. The learning process became more personalized as students interacted with their classmates over ideas and in ways that were personally more meaningful. They made connections to other parts of their knowledge base in ways that cannot be learned solely through a lecture. The learning groups also became a place where students could speak about ideas they did not yet fully understand. We really got a buzz as we heard them share their thoughts with others. They also discovered what they did not know.

Group learning can help students zero right in on their intellectual blind spots, showing them precisely what part of their thinking is unformed, flawed or confused. We found that these collaborative projects allowed students to experiment with ideas and then reflect, thus deepening their understanding of concepts. We also saw the students integrate new information into a more meaningful, coherent and defensible system. By such a construction of meaning, students made new information their own. Their contribution to lectures became more effective. The involvement of group members also produced more varied input, and here diversity can provide a distinct advantage: as students from different backgrounds contributed, discussions expanded and deepened; better and more creative decisions resulted.

Learning groups are appealing in part because they offer a broad range of possibilities. Depending on learning outcomes, group size may vary. We found five to seven members seemed best for ensuring equitable participation by everyone. The length of time you devote to any group activity can also vary. You may decide to incorporate a short activity as a change of pace within the context of a lecture, for example, or introduce a collaborative assignment that lasts the entire lecture period. In large classes where seats are bolted down, you can have students consult with others seated nearby or assign projects to be pursued for the most part outside the classroom. Weekly assignments or term projects can also be organized cooperatively.

Because students are often busy, you may have to help students get their groups started; for example, we scheduled a time and place for those who want to form study groups and used e-mail as a mechanism for linking students outside of class. For some cooperative projects, it is possible to divide the labour so that group members take responsibility for learning material or developing skills individually before coming back together to contribute to the whole. This technique, often used by students in study groups to manage their time more efficiently, has been dubbed 'the jigsaw' because each participant contributes an essential piece to the completed puzzle.

Using group learning, however, does not mean handing over full responsibility for a class to the students; rather, you temporarily surrender your role as sole expert and focus on designing and managing collaborative learning activities where students can be active in supporting one another's understanding. In this discussion, we cannot ignore the importance of the lecturer's role as manager of the group experience, or the time commitment that this can represent. We were used to more traditional lecturing, and found we needed to concentrate on a different set of skills for effective group facilitation. For example, we wanted to monitor groups closely so that workloads were distributed fairly and all students contributed to the communal effort. Some of our groups required regular supervision in order to keep on task. We also had to watch out for 'collaborative' misinformation where incorrect 'solutions' were passed around unchecked.

As for assessment, most faculty members who use cooperative learning establish mechanisms for measuring individual and group progress. If you decide to assign a group grade, you can expect a mixed response from students. On one hand, they will typically appreciate the support and assistance they receive from other group members but still hold one another accountable for the effort required and the mutual interdependence that motivates cooperative learning. On the other hand, we found some students understandably anxious about their dependence on others when their grade was on the line. While this anxiety can create tensions within groups, it can also promote greater effort and enhance performance, both collectively and individually.

There is no doubt that the group studies in Bill's introductory zoology course made the students more comfortable. Towards the end of the semester, many groups sat together and keeping them from talking was much more difficult. This relatively minor problem was mitigated by the fact that they were often (though not always) talking about the class material. It is worth noting that they were largely first-year students and their discomfort level and isolation at the beginning of class were palpable. Ours is a dauntingly huge university; students are often lonely and unstable, and a peer connection anchors them to the earth.

We had several excellent students, who said it was unfair to the student who prefers to work solo. Andy claimed that the group meetings were an inefficient use of students' time, becoming quite vociferous on the topic. The argument that the approach is unfair does not hold if you give the student the same handouts and opportunities to do the work on his/her own. We tried to talk the solo student into giving the group study a try, emphasizing the benefits of the group approach which are not limited to listening to others present their part; rather, the act of teaching others greatly facilitates learning the material.

In conclusion, in the two cases cited here, small cooperative learning groups provided an important addition to our traditional lecture classes. With some advance organization and ongoing supervision, students found that their work in teams helped them become more active learners within a large lecture format. Student engagement in these activities was infectious and the benefits of their interest and attentiveness flowed back to the lecturers, galvanizing an enhanced level of enthusiasm.

Despite these benefits, however, there are costs of time, focus and resources to consider. While every lecturer will have to sort out the costs and benefits on a course by course basis, it is hard to argue against some use of small cooperative groups within lectures. The benefit for us was a lecture room as interested and energized as any we have taught. Like the analogy we introduced at the beginning, lecturing by itself can leave students exhausted or bored with their largely passive role as passengers moving downriver. Organizing small, cooperative study groups can help students get off into tributaries, exploring small reflecting pools, promoting more active learning and deeper understanding.

REFERENCES

Timpson, W (1999) *Stepping Up: College learning and community for a sustainable future*, Atwood, Madison, Wisconsin

INSIGHTS FROM THE CASE STUDIES

The themes to emerge from the case studies in this book are both ancient and modern. Many of the difficulties and dilemmas presented are as old as teaching itself. However, the situations in which the dilemmas and difficulties emerged are often the product of modern-day policies in higher education. The angst described by case study authors stems from their desire to be the best possible lecturer in the circumstances. This closing chapter draws together some of the themes that emerge from the case studies presented in the book.

LEARNING OUTCOMES

A very strong message to come from a number of the case studies has been the value of being clear about what you are trying to achieve in a lecture. **Learning from Objectives** makes this quite explicit and a number of other cases also identify this as an important aspect of the story – **Playing the Crowded House, Teaching Power, Just Give Us the Right Answer, Getting to Know You, This is All Irrelevant!** While articulating and teaching to desired learning outcomes may seem obvious, even trite, it is an aspect of teaching that is often forgotten. There are a number of reasons for this. The traditional notion of the lecture focuses on content. The advent of 'hi-tech' lecture theatres and ubiquitous 'PowerPoint' presentations also tend to emphasize the delivery of content. Larger classes, greater diversity of students and less opportunity to get to know them mean lecturers become distanced from students and are less aware of their needs. The use of 'service teaching' can make articulating desired outcomes an area of contestation – **This is All Irrelevant!** And perhaps even more influential than any of these is the lack of training and preparation for university teachers – **New at This, The Smart Student, Getting to Know You**.

Articulating desired learning outcomes and teaching to them are the most basic and fundamental tasks in lecturing. They direct yet liberate the lecturer – **How Can I Lecture That Topic?** – and are the foundation on which all the other themes and activities in lecturing are built. Back to basics – articulating and teaching to desired learning outcomes – remains an important message to emerge from these case studies.

STUDENT ACTIVITIES AND PARTICIPATION

Research in learning and teaching in higher education emphasizes the fact that students construct meaning and need to be actively engaged in their own learning. Lecturers in turn can design their sessions to be interactive in order to encourage appropriate student learning. The lecture as a teaching method is changing from being a scene of information transmission to one of managing the active participation of students in learning. Many examples of this are evident in the case studies including **From Big Water to Reflective Pools, I Fell Asleep in My Own Lecture, Learning From the Inside Out, Just Give Us the Right Answer** and **We Might Have to Learn It but We Shouldn't Have to Think About It**.

Lecturers use activities that:

- demonstrate the values, ideals and concepts they want to teach, eg power, active discovery, controversial issues, critical thinking, alternative culture – **Teaching Power, I Fell Asleep in My Own Lecture, How Can I Lecture That Topic?, We Might Have to Learn It but We Shouldn't Have to Think About It, Learning From the Inside Out** and **Is it Me?**;
- help students learn from one another, eg study groups, role-plays, group work – **Just Give Us the Right Answer, From Big Water to Reflective Pools**;
- tap into alternative media or approaches, eg use of music, drawing, audiotapes – **Learning From the Inside Out, Clearly You Can't Do It**.

LISTENING AND RESPONDING TO STUDENT FEEDBACK

Feedback from students is a key source of information for lecturers to use in improving their courses and teaching. The case studies contain examples of feedback that is:

- formal and at the end of a course;
- systematic but collected during teaching time as opposed to the end of the course;
- unsolicited.

The first of these, feedback through formal university systems, is the most common feedback that lecturers collect. As the cases in this book show – **Is it Me?**, **This is All Irrelevant!**, **Getting to Know You** – such feedback can provoke major action and personal growth for lecturers as well as changes in learning for students.

But lecturers often want more immediate information that can be used to fine-tune an ongoing lecturing process. **Teaching Power** and **Playing the Crowded House** give good examples of how ongoing feedback can be collected systematically and how collection can be adapted for dealing with large numbers of students.

The third type of feedback is the immediate face-to-face feedback lecturers receive from students. This can be in the form of an unprovoked outburst – **Learning from Objectives, This is All Irrelevant!, We Might Have to Learn It but We Shouldn't Have to Think About It, Clearly You Can't Do It** – or in the lecturer's reading of more subtle clues – **New at This, Getting Sacked, Learning From the Inside Out**. Lecturers need to collect and deal with all three types of feedback.

Obtaining or receiving feedback is one thing, acting on it is another. Involving students in the process is important if students are to feel valued for their contribution and be without fear of retribution for the comments they make. All the lecturers in these case studies had the courage to tackle change based on feedback. Three aspects of acting on feedback stand out in the case studies:

- the loneliness of dealing with feedback – most lecturers did not have a safe and supportive place to go where they could deal with the emotional impact of critical feedback;
- the determination of lecturers to adjust their teaching in the light of student feedback;
- the repertoire of skills that lecturers had in dealing with crises, the ability to think on the spot and to make changes ranging from fine-tuning to major shifts.

Many lecturers dealing with feedback describe their reaction as 'intuitive'. It is in fact far more likely to be the product of skill, experience and artistry that remain largely unarticulated.

SERVING DIFFERENT INTERESTS

Particular difficulties arise for lecturers who find themselves serving different interests such as service teaching for a profession school – **This is All Irrelevant!, Getting to Know You, Is it Me?** – or meeting outside professional expectations – **The Smart Student, Learning from Objectives**.

Service teaching highlights epistemological issues for disciplines as they interface with other areas. There is often the assumption that moving across subject boundaries is easy and has minimum requirements for support or previous consultation. A change of perspective on how particular subject matter can be taught may be required, along with negotiation both within the teaching group and with 'the outside master'. The result can be insightful and transformative; the process often questions tacit assumptions about subject matter and teaching processes.

BEING AUTHENTIC

Many of the case study authors in this book have demonstrated that it is possible within the lecturing format to be true to deeply held values, living them through what is taught and how it is taught – **Teaching Power, How Can I Lecture That Topic?, Clearly You Can't Do It, Learning from the Inside Out**. This requires both a well-developed philosophy and the skills and capacity to turn it into a learning process for students. It is perhaps one of the hardest, or more advanced learning outcomes that lecturers might aim for with their students. The case studies here demonstrate the potential.

Another aspect of authenticity is acknowledgement that lecturing is an emotional business and getting negative feedback from students can add to the emotional load – **Just Give Us the Right Answer, Is it Me?, We Might Have to Learn It but We Shouldn't Have to Think About It, The Mobile Phone, The Smart Student, Getting Sacked**. Lecturing is also exhausting and can be essentially lonely for the teacher. One of the challenges for higher education is to acknowledge and deal with this reality in a positive and constructive way.

INSTITUTIONAL ISSUES

While lecturing is the backbone of university teaching, it is an activity left essentially to individual lecturers. These case studies highlight some the ways in which institutions fail to support their lecturers. For new staff there is often little or no support in the basics of lecturing and enhancing student learning – **New at This, The Smart Student, Getting to Know You**. Despite progress in some countries, training and qualification for lecturing staff are not yet a universal expectation. Teaching in universities is a professional activity and such lack of regard for required skills and competencies is, to say the least, surprising. A minimum requirement for universities that have concern for the quality of their teaching is training and support for new teaching staff.

Equally, staff in ongoing lecturing roles need support. In the case studies many lecturers felt isolated, alone and with no 'safe place' to work through the emotional impact of their situation and to be supported in their next steps – **We Might Have to Learn It but We Shouldn't Have to Think About It, Getting Sacked**. Where are the teams to work in? Where are the mentors? Where are the peer-feedback systems? Where is the collegial support when things are not going well? Supporting lecturers is the role of the whole academic community, with special responsibilities for heads of departments and course leaders. Alongside help from central or faculty-based education development centres, there are also a number of low-cost developmental processes that can be instigated, 'good practice days' and mentoring and peer appraisal, for example. These could support lecturers through emotionally traumatic teaching times, help to share good practice and contribute to raising the standard of teaching in general.

TEACHING ACCOMMODATION

There are issues concerning the space in which the lecturing takes place. Staff are severely constrained, and sometimes protected, by the spaces in which they are required to teach – **Playing the Crowded House, The Smart Student, New at This, Clearly You Can't Do It, Getting Sacked**. Lecture theatres in particular have a style of architecture that models one idea of the activity that will happen there – information transmission to a passive and confined audience. Both design features to accommodate larger numbers, and the addition of imposing banks of technology, have increased the separation of lecturers from their students. There are many ways we can improve on current architectural practices, such as ensuring new buildings or rooms have collaborative teams of lecturers and designers involved in the planning and design stage. This will enable expertise on both sides to be shared. As a higher education community we should be clamouring for better and more adaptive teaching spaces that are suitable for the teaching activities we wish to plan and implement.

FREEDOM

The final point that permeates all the cases is the freedom that lecturers have to adapt and change – **Getting to Know You, From Big Water to Reflective Ponds, The Mobile Phone, Playing the Crowded House, I Feel Asleep in My Own Lecture, Learning From Objectives** – to name only a few. While lecturing is regarded by many as a constrained and inflexible way of teaching, the reality as demonstrated through these cases is that lecturers have enormous possibilities and freedom within the format.

This is a major message of this book – the potential of the lecture to 'absorb' and use good features from a wide range of teaching and learning methods. There is clearly need to move away from the idea that a lecture is '50–55 minutes of largely uninterrupted discourse from a teacher with no discussion between students and no student activity other than listening and note-taking'. There is freedom and potential to lecture in ways that concentrate on learning rather than teaching and actively engage students.

We hope that you have been inspired by the case studies presented in this book and will take them on board in your own continuing professional journey. We trust you will find the freedom to reflect and change, as have the case reporters in this book.

FURTHER READING

Aylett, R and Gregory, K (1996) (ed) *Evaluating Teacher Quality in Higher Education*, Falmer Press, London

Beaty, L (1998) The professional development of teachers in higher education: Structures, methods and responsibilities, *Innovations in Education and Training International*, **35** (2), pp 99–107

Beerens, D R (2000) *Evaluating Teachers for Professional Growth: Creating a culture of motivation and learning*, Corwin Press, California

Bess, J L (1997) (ed) *Teaching Well and Liking It: Motivating faculty to teach effectively*, Johns Hopkins, London

Bess, J L (2000) *Teaching Alone and Teaching Together*, Jossey-Bass, San Francisco

Biggs, J (1999) *Teaching for Quality Learning at University*, SRHE and Open University Press, Buckingham

Biggs, J (1999) What the student does: Teaching for enhanced learning, *Higher Education Research and Development*, **18** (1), pp 55–75

Bligh, D A (2000) *What's the Use of Lectures?* Jossey-Bass, San Francisco

Bochner, D (1995) *Teaching More Students: 6: Supporting more students*, Oxford Centre for Staff Development, Oxford

Bonwell, C C (1991) *Active Learning: Creating excitement in the classroom*, ASHE-ERIC

Boud, D, Cohen, R and Walker, D (ed) (1996) *Using Experience for Learning*, SRHE and Open University Press, Buckingham

Bowden, J and Marton, F (1998) *The University of Learning: Beyond quality and competence in higher education*, Kogan Page, London

Brookfield, S D (1990) *Skillful Teacher: On technique, trust and responsiveness in the classroom*, Jossey-Bass, San Francisco

Brookfield, S D (1995) *Becoming a Critically Reflective Teacher*, Jossey-Bass, San Francisco

Brookfield, S D (1999) *Discussion as a Way of Teaching*, Jossey-Bass, San Francisco

Brown, G and Atkins, M (1988) *Effective Teaching in Higher Education*, Methuen, London

Brown, S and Smith, B (ed) (1996) *Resource-based Learning*, Kogan Page, London

Cannon, R and Newble, D (2000) *A Handbook for Teachers in Universities and Colleges*, 4th edn, Kogan Page, London

Carbone, E P (1998) *Teaching Large Classes: Tools and strategies*, Sage, London

Carrotte, P (1999) Turning academics into teachers: S Roland et al, *Teaching in Higher Education*, **4** (3), pp 411–13

Catt, R and Eke, J (1995) Classroom talk in higher education: Enabling learning through a reflective analysis of practice, *Innovations in Education and Training International*, **32** (4), pp 362–69

Centre for Learning and Teaching (1993) *Teaching Matters: Lectures*, video, University of Technology, Sydney

Chalmers, D and Fuller, R (1996) *Teaching for Learning at University*, Kogan Page, London

Cotton, J (1995) *The Theory of Learning Strategies: An introduction*, Kogan Page, London

Cowan, J (1998) *On Becoming an Innovative University Teacher: Reflection in action*, SRHE and Open University Press, Buckingham

Cox, B (1994) *Practical Pointers for University Teachers*, Kogan Page, London

Crebbin, W (1997) Defining quality teaching in higher education: An Australian perspective, *Teaching in Higher Education*, **2** (1), pp 21–32

Cross, P (1996) *Classroom Research: Implementing the scholarship of teaching*, Jossey-Bass, San Francisco

Cryer, P and Elton, L (1992) *Active Learning in Large Classes and with Increasing Students Numbers*, CVCP Universities' Staff Development and Training Unit, Sheffield

Day, K, Grant, R and Hounsell, D (1998) *Reviewing Your Teaching*, Centre for Teaching Learning and Assessment, University of Edinburgh, Edinburgh

Dijk, L A v, Berg, G C v d and Keulen, H v (1999) Using active instructional methods in lectures: A matter of skills and preferences, *Innovations in Education and Training International*, **36** (4), pp 260–72

Elton, L (1998) Dimensions of excellence in university teaching, *The International Journal for Academic Development*, **3** (1), pp 3–11

Entwhistle, N J (1988) *Styles of Learning and Teaching*, David Fulton, London

Forsyth, I (1999) *Evaluating a Course*, 2nd edn, Kogan Page, London

Fry, H, Ketteridge, S and Marshall, S (ed) (1999) *A Handbook of Teaching and Learning in Higher Education: Enhancing academic practice*, Kogan Page, London

Gibbs, G (1992) *Improving the Quality of Students Learning*, Technical and Educational Services Ltd, Bristol

Gibbs, G (1992) *Teaching More Students: 1: Problems and course design strategies*, Oxford Centre for Staff Development, Oxford

Gibbs, G (1992) *Teaching More Students: 2: Lecturing to more students*, Oxford Centre for Staff Development, Oxford

Gibbs, G, Habeshaw, S and Habeshaw, T (1992) *53 Interesting Things to do in Your Lectures*, Technical and Educational Services Ltd, Bristol

Gibbs, G and Jenkins, A (ed) (1992) *Teaching Large Classes in Higher Education*, Kogan Page, London

Habeshaw, S, Gibbs, G and Habeshaw, T (1992) *53 Problems with Large Classes: Making the best of a bad job*, Technical and Educational Services Ltd, Bristol

Halliday, J, and Soden, R (1998) Facilitating changes in lecturers' understanding of learning, *Teaching in Higher Education*, 3 (1), pp 21–35

Higgs, J and Edwards, H (1999) *Educating Beginning Practitioners: Challenges for health professional education*, Butterworth Heinemann, Oxford

Hounsell, D, Tait, H and Day, K (1997) *Feedback on Courses and Programmes of Study*, Centre for Teaching Learning and Assessment University of Edinburgh, Edinburgh

Kember, D (2000) *Action Learning and Action Research: Improving the quality of teaching and learning*, Kogan Page, London

Laurillard, D (1993) *Rethinking University Teaching*, Routledge, London

Leach, J, and Moon, B (ed) (1999) *Learners and Pedagogy*, Paul Chapman Publishing and Open University, London

Leamnson, R (1999) *Thinking about Teaching and Learning*, Trentham, Stoke-on-Trent

McKeachie, W J (1999) *McKeachie's Teaching Tips: Strategies, research and theory for college and university teachers*, Houghton Mifflin Co, Boston

Melton, R F (1997) *Objectives, Competencies and Learning Outcomes*, Kogan Page, London

Moon, J (1999) *Reflection in Learning and Professional Development: Theory and practice*, Kogan Page, London

Neill, S and Caswell, C (1993) *Body Language for Competent Teachers*, Routledge, London

Nilson, L B (1998) *Teaching at its Best: A research-based resource for college instructors*, Anker, Bolton, MA

Palmer, P (1998) *The Courage to Teach*, Jossey-Bass, San Francisco

Perry, R P and Smart J C (ed) (1997) *Effective Teaching in Higher Education: Research and practice*, Agathon Press, New York

Prosser, M and Trigwell K (1998) *Understanding Learning and Teaching*, Open University Press, Buckingham

Race, P (1993) *Never Mind the Teaching Feel the Learning*, SEDA, Birmingham

Race, P (ed) (1999) *2000 Tips for Lecturers*, Kogan Page, London

Race, P, and Brown, S (1998) *The Lecturer's Toolkit: A practical guide to teaching learning and assessment*, Kogan Page, London

Ramsden, P (1992) *Learning to Teach in Higher Education*, Routledge, London

Riding, R, and Raynor, S (1998) *Cognitive Styles and Learning Strategies: Understanding style differences in learning and behaviour*, David Fulton, London

Rowland, S *et al* (1998) Turning academics into teachers? *Teaching in Higher Education*, 3 (2), pp 133–41

Seldin, P (1999) *Changing Practices in Evaluating Teaching: A practical guide*, Anker, Bolton, MA

Shulman, L S (1999) Taking learning seriously, *Change*, **31** (4), pp 11–17

Smeby, J C (1998) Knowledge production and knowledge transmission: The interaction between research and teaching, *Teaching in Higher Education*, 3 (1), pp 5–20

Smith, B (1997) *Lecturing to Large Groups*, SEDA, Birmingham

Smith, B and Brown, S (ed) (1995) *Research Teaching and Learning in Higher Education*, Kogan Page, London

Squires, G (1999) *Teaching as a Professional Discipline*, Falmer Press, London

Webb, G (1994) *Making the Most of Your Appraisal*, Kogan Page, London

Whisker, G and Brown, S (ed) (1996) *Enabling Student Learning*, Kogan Page, London

Whittock, T (1997) Reflexive teaching, reflexive learning, *Teaching in Higher Education*, 2 (2), pp 93–102

INDEX